GLOBALIZATION AND
SOCIAL MOVEMENTS

D0217369

GLOBALIZATION

Series Editors

Manfred B. Steger
*Royal Melbourne Institute of Technology and
University of Hawai'i–Mānoa*
and
Terrell Carver
University of Bristol

"Globalization" has become *the* buzzword of our time. But what does it mean? Rather than forcing a complicated social phenomenon into a single analytical framework, this series seeks to present globalization as a multidimensional process constituted by complex, often contradictory interactions of global, regional, and local aspects of social life. Since conventional disciplinary borders and lines of demarcation are losing their old rationales in a globalizing world, authors in this series apply an interdisciplinary framework to the study of globalization. In short, the main purpose and objective of this series is to support subject-specific inquiries into the dynamics and effects of contemporary globalization and its varying impacts across, between, and within societies.

 Supported by the Globalization Research Center at the University of Hawai'i, Mānoa

GLOBALIZATION AND SOCIAL MOVEMENTS

ISLAMISM, FEMINISM, AND THE GLOBAL JUSTICE MOVEMENT

VALENTINE M. MOGHADAM

ROWMAN & LITTLEFIELD PUBLISHERS, INC.
Lanham • Boulder • New York • Toronto • Plymouth, UK

ROWMAN & LITTLEFIELD PUBLISHERS, INC.

Published in the United States of America
by Rowman & Littlefield Publishers, Inc.
A wholly owned subsidary of The Rowman & Littlefield Publishing Group, Inc.
4501 Forbes Boulevard, Suite 200, Lanham, Maryland 20706
www.rowmanlittlefield.com

Estover Road, Plymouth PL6 7PY, United Kingdom

British Library Cataloguing in Publication Information Available

Library of Congress Cataloging-in-Publication Data

Moghadam, Valentine M., 1952–
   Globalization and social movements : Islamism, feminism, and the global justice
movement / Valentine M. Moghadam.
      p. cm. — (Globalization)
   Includes bibliographical references and index.
   ISBN-13: 978-0-7425-5571-6 (cloth : alk. paper)
   ISBN-10: 0-7425-5571-2 (cloth : alk. paper)
   ISBN-13: 978-0-7425-5572-3 (pbk. : alk. paper)
   ISBN-10: 0-7425-5572-0 (pbk. : alk. paper)
   [etc.]
   1. Social movements. 2. Transnationalism. 3. Globalization. I. Title.
HM881.M64 2009
303.48'409—dc22

                                                                          2008030174

Printed in the United States of America

∞ ™ The paper used in this publication meets the minimum requirements of
American National Standard for Information Sciences—Permanence of Paper
for Printed Library Materials, ANSI/NISO Z39.48-1992.

CONTENTS

FIGURES AND TABLES

FIGURE

TABLES

PREFACE

This book originates in an invitation extended by Manfred Steger when we were both at Illinois State University and he had just taken on the co-editorship of this book series. It took me several years to finally begin the project, and I am grateful to Manfred, and to the other series editor Terrell Carver and acquisitions editor Susan McEachern, for their patience, encouragement, and support. I also wish to thank the anonymous reader for very helpful comments.

The topic of this book is globalization and transnational social movements. I define *globalization* as a complex economic, political, cultural, and geographic process in which the mobility of capital, peoples, organizations, movements, ideas, and discourses takes on an increasingly transnational or global form. The Internet—a "gift" of globalization—has made possible rapid communication, transfers, and mobilizations. And yet, the type of economic globalization that has emerged is *neoliberal capitalist*, with its features of denationalization, privatization, flexible labor markets, and deregulated capital markets. Among its deficits is attention to labor rights, human rights, women's rights, and environmental protection. It thus devolves upon activists, mobilized in local or transnational networks, to form movements for change. Thus just as globalization has engendered the spread of neoliberal capitalism across the world, it also has stoked opposition and collective action. And while the Internet has allowed capitalists to speculate, buy, and sell across space and time, it also allows activists to organize and mobilize rapidly and effectively.

We are living in times of insecurity, instability, and risk, but equally in times of opportunity and possibility. Climate change, war, and economic recession loom large, while increased militarization by states and violent contention by non-state actors contribute to a seemingly dangerous world. But these developments have been met by sustained opposition and mobilization for change: the transformation of the status quo and the building of "another world" that is peaceful, environmentally sound, and egalitarian. Networks and communities of activists across borders—notably feminists, environmentalists, human rights advocates, and economic justice activists who constitute *transnational social movements*—have initiated sustained critiques of the contemporary world-system and have offered rational and feasible alternatives.

This book is dedicated to all such activists.

ACRONYMS

AKP	Justice and Development Party (Turkey)
ATTAC	Association to Tax Financial Transactions to Aid Citizens
AWID	Association for Women's Rights in Development
CEDAW	Convention on the Elimination of all Forms of Discrimination Against Women; also: Committee on the Elimination of Discrimination Against Women (UN)
COSATU	Congress of South African Trade Unions
DAWN	Development Alternatives with Women for a New Era
ECOSOC	Economic and Social Committee (UN)
ENDA	Environnement et Développement du Tiers-monde
EU	European Union
FIS	Front Islamique du Salut (Islamic Salvation Front, Algeria)
FTAA	Free Trade Area of the Americas
GIA	Groupe Armée Islamique
GJM	global justice movement
IAW	International Alliance of Women
ICFTU	International Confederation of Free Trade Unions
ICPD	UN International Conference on Population and Development (Cairo, 1994)
IGO	inter-governmental organization
IGTN	International Gender and Trade Network
ILO	International Labor Organization (UN)
IMF	International Monetary Fund
INGO	international non-governmental organization
IROWS	Institute for Research on World-Systems

ISIS	International Women's Information and Communication Service
MAI	Multilateral Agreement on Investment
MDS	Movement of Socialist Democrats
NAFTA	North American Free Trade Association
NATO	North Atlantic Treaty Organization
NGO	non-governmental organization
NIEO	New International Economic Order
OECD	Organization for Economic Cooperation and Development
PAS	Pan-Malaysian Islamic Party/Parti Islam Se-Malaysia
PJD	Parti du Justice et Dévéloppement (Morocco)
PT	Partido dos Trabalhadores (Workers' Party, Brazil)
SAP	structural adjustment policy
SIGI	Sisterhood Is Global Institute
SMO	social movement organization
TCC	transnational capitalist class
TFN	transnational feminist network
UNCTAD	United Nations Conference on Trade and Development
UNCED	UN Conference on Environment and Development
UNDP	United Nations Development Programme
UNU	United Nations University
WEDO	Women's Environment and Development Organization
WICEJ	Women's International Coalition for Economic Justice
WIDE	Network Women in Development in Europe
WIDF	Women's International Democratic Federation
WILPF	Women's International League for Peace and Freedom
WLP	Women's Learning Partnership
WLUML	Women Living Under Muslim Laws
WSF	World Social Forum
WTO	World Trade Organization

CHAPTER 1

INTRODUCTION AND OVERVIEW

What is the connection between globalization and social movements? How have people collectively responded to globalization? Have social movements changed to better confront globalization's economic, political, and cultural manifestations and challenges? And how are contemporary social movements and networks affecting the progression of globalization? These are the principal questions posed and addressed in this book, through a focus on three transnational or global social movements: the global women's movement and transnational feminist networks; transnational Islamist movements and networks; and the global justice movement. In addition to exploring the mutual relationship between globalization and social movements, this book examines the ways that the social sciences have sought to address changing social realities.

The social sciences have long focused on processes and institutions within single states, societies, and economies. Until the 1990s, the terms "global" and "transnational" represented concepts that were either alien or marginal to mainstream social-science theories. "International" and "world" were of course understood, but supra-national developments could hardly be fathomed. The Cold War world order consisted of the First World, Second World, and Third World—also known as the rich capitalist countries of the West, the countries of the communist bloc, and the developing countries of Africa, Asia, and Latin America—and while scholars studied these political and economic regions, analyses tended to focus on single societies and economies. Dependency theory and its more sophisticated variant, world-system theory, challenged mainstream social science theorizing as well as Marxism's emphasis on class conflicts within single societies, drawing attention to the transnational nature of capital and labor flows and the implications thereof for economic and political processes at the societal level, as well as for the reproduction of global inequalities.[1] (However, in *The Communist Manifesto*, Karl Marx and Friedrich Engels were absolutely correct in predicting the ever-growing concentration of capital and its expansion across the globe.) World-system theory in particular was unique in its conceptual and methodological approach. Though it posited the existence of hierarchical "economic zones" of core, periphery, and semi-periphery, it insisted that the analytical point of departure should be the structures of the world-system in its entirety. Back in the mainstream, theories of social movements and "new social movements" focused on national-level dynamics— and mainly in the West or in "post-industrial society."[2] But no sooner had these theories gained prominence in the 1980s than new developments began to challenge some of their basic assumptions.

The new developments included forms of governance and activism on a world scale, as well as global shifts in political economy. New governance structures included the ever-growing power and influence of multinational corporations, the World Bank, the International Monetary Fund (IMF), and (later) the World Trade Organization (WTO), along with the emergence of regional blocs such as the European Union (EU) and the North American Free Trade Agreement (NAFTA). These institutions of global and regional governance were also behind shifts in the international political economy, which entailed the move from Keynesian or state-directed economic models to neoliberal or free-market economic strategies. Thus the "structural adjustment and stabilization" policies that were advocated for indebted Third World countries during the 1980s and 1990s, the transition from socialism to capitalism in the Second World, and the free-market imprint of Reaganism and Thatcherism in the First World all seemed to be part of a global process of economic restructuring.[3] Along with these changes arose a powerful ideology of free market capitalism and consumerism.[4]

As globalization was being observed in its economic, political, and cultural dimensions, some scholars came to analyze what they viewed as a global tendency toward common values. Echoing some arguments made earlier by modernization theorists, proponents of "world society" maintained that certain structures, institutions, and processes are explicit or implicit carriers of modern values such as rationality and individuality. These carriers include rationalized state tax and management systems, formal organizations, bureaucratized legal systems, and formal schooling. In the 1990s, emphasis began to be placed on the role of international organizations in the construction of world values. World polity theory places primacy on cultural and political institutions and norms, emphasizing norm diffusion and convergences in political and cultural developments, which is interpreted as a kind of global westernization. It posits a tendency toward isomorphism in institutions, values, practices, and norms across the globe, indicated by adoption by states of all manner of international instruments, along with the exponential growth and increased prominence of national and international non-governmental organizations. Theorists argued that there was thus movement toward "world culture" and a kind of "world polity." In this perspective, world culture encourages countries to adopt similar strategies for addressing common problems. World organizations are viewed as "primary instruments of shared modernity," disseminating standards and practices, and international conventions and treaties often provide declarations of common causes and blueprints for change. Social movements and civil society organizations—including human rights and women's rights associations, environmental protection groups, and so on—are regarded as active agents in the deepening of the cultural and normative features of world society.[5]

Parallel to the economic shifts that were unfolding in the 1970s and 1980s, a new phenomenon occurred that the theorists of new social movements had some difficulty addressing, focused as they were on presumed emancipatory, post-class, and post-ideological new social movements in the democratic West: the rise and spread of Islamic fundamentalist movements in the Middle East, North Africa, and South Asia that sought to curb Western political and cultural influences and recuperate traditional social and gender norms. The theorization of these movements fell largely on scholars within Middle East studies and Middle East women's studies, although Benjamin Barber later included them under the rubric of "jihad" movements against "McWorld."[6]

Another apparent outcome of globalization and a challenge to conventional theories of social movements was the rise in the late 1990s of what have been variously called transnational advocacy networks, transnational social movements, and global social movements. Social movement theorists previously had focused on domestic processes and movement characteristics, but it became increasingly clear that the analytical point of departure would have to take account of the transnational, and that local–global linkages would have to be theorized. Early theorists of transnational advocacy networks focused on ideational and ethical motivations for the emergence of the human rights, environmental, and solidarity movements,[7] but the 1997–1998 mobilization against the Multilateral Agreement on Investment (MAI) and the Battle of Seattle in late 1999 confirmed that movement interest in economic, inequality, and class issues had returned. A new body of literature emerged, therefore, taking these novel departures into consideration. There is now some consensus among scholars that the response to global economic, political, and cultural developments has taken the form of transnational collective action, including the emergence of transnational social movements and advocacy networks that focus on human rights, the environment, and economic justice.

A transnational social movement has come to be understood as a mass mobilization uniting people in three or more countries, engaged in sustained contentious interactions with political elites, international organizations, or multinational corporations.[8] Thus a transnational social movement is analytically distinct from, though related to, an international solidarity network or a transnational advocacy network. For Keck and Sikkink, a transnational advocacy network (TAN) is a set of "relevant actors working internationally on an issue who are bound together by shared values, a common discourse and dense exchanges of information and services. . . . Activists in networks try not only to influence policy outcomes but to transform the terms and nature of the debate."[9] Such networks typically identify themselves with social movements, such as feminism, environmentalism, human rights, or peace and justice. Transnational social movements and transnational advocacy networks alike are structurally linked to globalization, and they constitute important sectors within global civil society.

Along with such forms of collective action, new transnational political spaces have opened, in the form of the World Social Forum and the regional forums. These are regarded as key institutions of at least two transnational social movements: the global justice movement and the global feminist movement. Whereas theorists of "new social movements" had projected feminist movements as localized and identity-focused, the 1990s saw women organizing and mobilizing across borders in transnational feminist networks, particularly around the effects of economic restructuring, patriarchal fundamentalisms, and violence against women.[10]

In the new millennium, therefore, a growing body of literature was examining both globalization processes and transnational social movements. At the same time, the attacks of September 11, 2001, broadened the scope of the study of Islamist movements beyond the purview of area specialists. Conventional social scientists became interested in analyzing militant Islam and the "war on terror," while the 2003 invasion of Iraq by the United States and Great Britain spurred numerous studies on war, "empire," and the new imperialism. These developments are pertinent to the study of globalization and social movements because they present questions about opportunities and resources for movement-building, the use of violence in social movements and transnational networks, the relationship of war to the global capitalist order, and the salience of masculinities in global processes.

This book integrates a discussion of theories and empirical documentation of social movements in an era of globalization while also offering an explanatory framework. It examines the relationship between globalization (in its economic, political, and cultural manifestations) and social movements, including the new forms of transnational collective action. The empirical chapters focus on three transnational social movements that emerged under the conditions of late capitalism/neoliberal globalization: the women's movement, political Islam, and the global justice movement. Undoubtedly, these are among the most vocal and visible of transnational movements and networks, and the choice of the three is indicative of the salience of normative issues and collective identities as well as structural causes. Each constitutes a transnational social movement inasmuch as it connects people across borders around a common agenda and collective identity; mobilizes large numbers of supporters and activists, whether as individuals or as members of networks, groups, and organizations; and engages in sustained oppositional politics with states or other power-holders. Despite this overarching similarity, however, what will become apparent in the course of this book is that although Islamist movements are internally differentiated, the grievances, methods, and goals of Islamist movements differ in profound ways from those of the non-violent radical democratic or socialist visions of global feminism and the global justice movement. One key difference is that many Islamist movements seek state power and, like revolutionary movements before them, are willing to use violence to achieve this aim. In contrast, both the feminist movement and the global justice movement are disinterested in state power, although they do seek wide-ranging institutional and normative changes, and they eschew violence.

ORIGINS AND ANTECEDENTS

Transnational social movements date back to the late eighteenth century, although in recent decades the scope of transnationalization and the scale of international ties among activists have risen dramatically. Sidney Tarrow has noted that social movements emerged in the eighteenth century from "structural changes that were associated with capitalism" such as "new forms of association, regular communication linking center and periphery, and the spread of print and literacy."[11] Social movements—like revolutions—are thus associated with modernity and capitalism; they are rooted in and are triggered by the contradictions of the capitalist world-system. In a Marxian dialectical sense, these contradictions entail both oppressive conditions and opportunities for action, resistance, and change. In her study of historical resistance to economic globalization, Zahara Heckscher identifies five episodes between the 1780s and the early 1900s: the Tupac Amaru II uprising in what is now Peru against the Spanish colonialists; the international movement against the Atlantic slave trade; European workers and the First International Workingman's Association; the campaign against the colonization of the Congo; and United States–Philippines solidarity in the anti-imperialist movement of the late nineteenth century.[12] These cases of what world-system analysts call "anti-systemic resistance" confirm Marx's apposite observation about structure and agency: "Men make history," he noted, "but not under conditions of their own choosing."

The choice of the global justice, Islamist, and feminist movements is not accidental. Apart from the fact that they are among the most prominent and visible of contemporary social movements, they also have historical antecedents in the eighteenth, nineteenth, and early twentieth centuries. The global justice movement of today can be linked back to transnational movements of workers, socialists, communists, progressives, and anarchists during an economic period that Karl Polanyi called the "great transformation."[13] Many of the older activists in the contemporary global justice movement were once affiliated with left-wing organizations or solidarity movements; many of the younger activists are involved in labor and economic justice causes; and the writings of Karl Marx are well known to many activists. Human rights groups also abound in the global justice movement, and some scholars have found similarities between their moral discourse, tactics, and strategies and those of the much earlier anti-slavery movement in the United States and the United Kingdom. Political scientists Margaret Keck and Kathryn Sikkink have noted that the backbone of the anti-slavery movement was made up of Quakers and the "dissenting denominations"—Methodists, Presbyterians, and Unitarians—who used reportage, conferences, and novels to push for abolition.[14] These tactics are still used in the human rights movement and in the global justice movement in general.

The Islamist movements that burst onto the international scene in the late 1970s and spread in the 1980s were rooted in eighteenth-, nineteenth-, and early twentieth-century revival movements, which in turn claimed to be following the path taken by the Prophet Muhammad in the seventh century A.D. Sociologist Mansoor Moaddel has traced the evolution of Islamic modernism, liberal nationalism, and Islamic fundamentalism, arguing that these movements arose in the context of different global developments, resources, cultural capital, and institutional ties. In advancing the proposition that "ideological production is a discontinuous process and proceeds in an episodic fashion," Moaddel elucidates the roots of contemporary fundamentalism or political Islam.[15] Hugh Roberts has shown how Algeria's Front Islamique du Salut (FIS) was part of the legacy of orthodox, urban-based Islamic reformists associated with the salafists of the early decades of the twentieth century against rural-based maraboutic Islam.[16] John Voll identified contemporary Islamic fundamentalism in Egypt and the Sudan with eighteenth- and nineteenth-century Wahhabist and Mahdist movements.[17] Today's Islamists are inspired by the rigid and puritanical legacies of Ibn Taymiyyah, a medieval Hanbali jurist, and Ibn Abd-al-Wahhab, an eighteenth-century theologian who formed an alliance with Muhammad Ibn Saud and built a religio-political movement that was defeated by the Ottomans but in the twentieth century formed the foundation of the new state of Saudi Arabia. Other sources of inspiration and guidance are the writings of Abul Ala Mawdudi (who founded the Jamiat-e Islami in India in 1941), the Egyptians Rashid Rida and Hassan al-Banna (who founded the Muslim Brotherhood in 1929), and Sayyid Qutb, all of whom took issue with modernity as it was proceeding in their countries and called for a return to strict implementation of sharia law. Sayyid Qutb's 1948–1950 stay in the United States convinced him that the *jahiliyya*—the so-called age of darkness that characterized pre-Islamic Arabia—had returned and needed to be combated. Today's militant Islamists use this term to describe the state of the world and justify their aggressive tactics. From Ibn Taymiyyah they adopted the duty to wage jihad against apostates and unbelievers.[18]

Islamist movements became prominent in the 1980s, but clearly Islam had been a mobilizing frame in decades before. Both Islamic and nationalist frames were used in anti-colonial struggles, but Islamist groups occasionally opposed progressive nationalist leaders. Thus in the 1950s, Iran's Premier Mossadegh and Egypt's Gamal Abdel Nasser incurred the opposition, respectively, of Sheikh Fazlollah Nouri and the Muslim Brotherhood.

The contemporary global women's movement has roots in first-wave feminism, with its focus on suffrage and justice for women, and in second-wave feminism, with its demands for equality and cultural change. First-wave feminism brought about international women's organizations around abolition, women's suffrage, opposition to trafficking in women, anti-militarism, and labor legislation for working women and mothers. In the United States, the 1840 Seneca Falls Convention was comprised of elite women familiar with the details of the French and American revolutions and supportive of the abolition movement. First-wave feminism later grew to include women disappointed that the franchise was not extended to them when (male) slaves were emancipated and given the right to vote. Scholars have identified moderate, socialist, and militant strands of the early feminist movement. Social movement organizations included the International Woman Suffrage Association (IWSA), formed in 1904. Its methods included speaking tours and rallies, but militants were ready to be arrested, jailed, and force-fed for the cause. Militant suffragists in the United States and the United Kingdom deployed public agitation, civil disobedience, and violent tactics to draw attention to their cause; these methods were used by the Women's Social and Political Union in the United Kingdom and by Alice Paul and her associates in the United States.

The early twentieth century also saw the emergence of an international socialist women's movement. In 1900 the Socialist International passed its first resolution in favor of women's suffrage, and suffrage became a demand of socialist parties in 1907. Within the Second International, the women's organizations of France, Germany, and Russia mobilized thousands of working-class as well as middle-class women for socialism and women's emancipation.[19] In Asian countries, as Kumari Jayawardena showed, many of the women's movements and organizations that emerged were associated with socialist or nationalist movements.[20] Although feminists and leftists have not always agreed on priorities or strategies, there has been a long-standing affinity that helps to explain the involvement of feminists in the global justice movement today. Examples of early international women's organizations are the Women's International League for Peace and Freedom (WILPF), the International Council of Women (ICW), the International Alliance of Women (IAW), the Women's International Democratic Federation (WIDF), and the Young Women's Christian Association (YWCA). In promoting women's rights, maternity legislation, and an end to child labor, they engaged with inter-governmental bodies such as the League of Nations and the International Labor Organization.[21]

THE WORLD-SYSTEM AND
SOCIAL MOVEMENTS

As noted, world-system theory posits the existence of a hierarchical inter-state system of unequal states and markets, with a hegemon (the dominant power, economically, politically, and militarily) and economic zones of core, periphery, and semi-periphery.[22] In the 1950s, the United States supplanted the United Kingdom as the world-system's hegemon. Scholars have argued that American economic power declined relatively after the 1970s—that is, relative to the growing power of Europe, the newly industrializing countries, and, more recently, China. Beginning with the Reagan administration, so the argument goes, successive American administrations sought to maintain American hegemony through diplomacy and free trade, including the so-called Washington Consensus that resulted in the spread of neoliberalism throughout the world. Debates among scholars ensue, however, over whether we are observing a new phase of U.S. imperialism, or the consolidation of an integrated system of global capitalism, or a combination of imperial and neoliberal projects.[23] Immanuel Wallerstein argues that the current world-system is in crisis and in a stage of transition, the end product of which is unknown and cannot be predicted.[24]

As the world-system is the primary unit of analysis, the position of a national state within one or another of the world-system's economic zones, and the relationship between the state in question and the hegemonic power, can shape the emergence, course, and consequences of social movements. Social movements in the democratic countries of the core may have more freedom to operate, mobilize resources, and express dissent, while those in peripheral or semi-peripheral countries may lack adequate resources and face considerably more repression. Similarly, participation in the global justice movement may be shaped by world-systemic constraints: networks and organizations from richer countries are likely to be involved in a more sustained manner and in greater numbers than are those from poorer countries. The world-system also affects social movements in the way that it generates grievances. The global justice movement, for example, has emerged precisely to challenge the dominance of a neoliberal world order and to call for "another world." And Islamist movements not only oppose aspects of what they see as a westernized and anti-Islamic modernity in their own countries but also take exception to the hegemonic power of the United States and its unwavering support for Israel's conduct with Palestinians and neighboring countries.

Social movement analysis has taken a clear theoretical shape within sociology. Scholars have long shown that the roots of social protest, organizing, and movement building are located in broad social change processes that destabilize existing power relations and increase the leverage of challenging groups. There is now an appreciation for the interconnection of political, organizational, and cultural processes in social movements, with scholars arguing that the three factors play roles of varying analytic importance over the course of the movement.[25] Opportunities are critical to emergence, as they are tied to the relative openness or closure of the political system and the state, the stability of the elite, and the presence or absence of elite allies. Pertinent questions are: How does the national political system influence movements? How does movement strategy and structure change in response to political opportunities? How do movements act within, and help create, political opportunities? Mobilizing structures—networks, associations, and patterns of recruitment, leadership, and resource mobilization—become more central as the movement develops. Much research has documented the formation and evolution of social movement organizations (SMOs), but research also shows that these originate in small groups or informal networks. Framing processes—the meanings given to action, the formation of collective identities, the ways in which issues are presented—are always important, but they become more self-conscious and tactical over the course of the movement. Scholars also have identified an ongoing process of "frame alignment," whereby social movement actors link their claims to interested audiences, often to strategically construct more resonant and persuasive frames that will mobilize people.[26]

The three aspects of social movements are interrelated, inasmuch as the structure of political opportunities can affect resource mobilization; meanings, frames, and identities can be formed in connection with available opportunities, resources, and audiences; and the political context can be influenced or even changed by concerted collective action. In addition, scholars examine cycles and waves of protest, and "collective action repertoires" such as boycotts, mass petitioning, marches, rallies, barricading, and acts of civil disobedience. To this list we should add the meetings and conferences typical of feminist action and the suicide bombings deployed by radical Islamists. While theorists continue to view social movements as a collective response to deprivation, to the contradictions of late capitalism, or to the availability of resources, the consensus that emerged in the 1990s stresses political processes but also views structural and cultural processes as key to understanding the strategies and cycles of social protest.

All movements have some structure, but not all movements have major formal organizations that dominate and direct movement activity. According to Luther Gerlach, social movements are "segmentary, polycentric, and reticulate." Illustrating his SPR thesis by way of the environmental movement, he shows that social movements have many, sometimes competing, organizations and groups (segmentary); they have multiple and sometimes competing leaders (polycentric); and they are loose networks that link to each other (reticulate). Despite the segmentation, however, there is a shared opposition and ideology. In the environmental movement, for example, SMOs have ranged from the very radical Earth First! to Greenpeace and Germany's Greens (who later evolved into the Green Party). Gerlach argues that the SPR nature of SMOs is very effective, allowing them to be flexible and adaptive, and to resonate with larger constituencies through different tactics (for example, direct action versus lobbying and legal strategies). It also "promotes striving, innovation, and entrepreneurial experimentation in generating and implementing sociocultural change."[27] This argument is relevant to all three of the movements that we examine in this book. Moreover, the type of mobilizing structures found in the global Islamist, feminist, and justice movements include not only formal organizations but also more fluid networks—and in the case of the Islamist movement, cells that act independently of any larger or more formal organization.

Combining the conceptual frameworks of the world-system and social movements helps us to better grasp the factors behind the emergence of the transnational social movements under consideration in this book, their characteristics, and their prospects. And integrating feminist insights allows us to discern the role of gender, and especially of hyper-masculinities, in so-cial movement dynamics and in specific tactics and strategies.

In this book, we discuss the opportunities, mobilizing structures, and frames pertinent to the global justice, Islamist, and feminist movements. (See table 1.1 for an elaboration.) But the role of emotions is important, too, as a growing body of literature points out.[28] Commitment, zeal, moral outrage, solidarity, ethics—these are aspects of social movement building and participation that scholars oriented toward rational choice theorizing have neglected. No one who examines Islamist movements can deny that there are strong emotional undercurrents and motivations among partici-pants. And when Muslim-owned media such as al-Jazeera and al-Arabiyya dwell on bombings in Afghanistan, Iraq, Lebanon, and Palestine, this can be regarded as a movement event that is also an emotion-producing ritual. Similarly, emotions play a role in the feminist and global justice move-ments. Violence against women is sometimes addressed analytically by feminists but often confronted in emotive terms. Activists within the global justice movement frequently articulate their opposition to neoliberal capi-talism and the international financial institutions in moral economy terms. Social movement actors do not simply engage in cool-headed cost-benefit calculations, but also express strong feelings about injustices and entitle-ments. Nor are these expressions limited to anger, alienation, and moral outrage. At anti-globalization protests and demonstrations there is often satire, parody, music, even puppetry—indeed, a festival-like atmosphere. Emotions such as joy, anger, commitment, and solidarity are as important in the social movement experience as the "entrepreneurial" dimensions.

For these reasons, elements of the older explanatory frameworks that focused on socio-psychological factors in protest mobilizations cannot be entirely ruled out as anachronistic or unhelpful. Indeed, the concept of cul-tural framing is rooted in social psychology. Moreover, the presence of emotions such as humiliation, anger, and frustration has been widely noted in connection with Muslim militants, by observers as well as by Islamists themselves. Osama bin Laden, for example, once declared that for over eighty years Islam had been "tasting . . . humiliation and contempt . . . its sons . . . killed; its blood . . . shed, its holy places . . . attacked."[29]

The assumptions, main arguments, and key concepts presented in this book can be summarized as the following:

1. Globalization is a multifaceted process of social change with eco-nomic, political, and cultural dimensions that reflect homogeneity

Table 1.1. Social Movement Features of Feminist, Islamist, and Global Justice Movements

	Opportunities and Resources	Mobilizing Structures: Networks and SMOs	Frames
Feminist	Socio-demographics: education and employment UN Decade for Women (1976–1985) and 1990s UN conferences Resources: women's organizations, donor agencies, European foundations	DAWN, WIDE, WLUML, WEDO, WILPF, Madre, WLP, Code Pink	Women's rights are human rights; end feminization of poverty; end violence against women; empowerment; gender justice; gender mainstreaming
Islamist			
• Parliamentarian	Local support; resources from Muslim states (Iran, Saudi Arabia, Libya); publicity and support via Arab media	Hamas, Hezbollah, Muslim Brotherhood	Islam is the solution; establish sharia law; end repression; justice for Palestine
• Extremist	U.S.-sponsored Afghan war, 1980–1992; resources from Muslim states; personal wealth; publicity via al-Jazeera	Al-Qaeda and affiliates	"Crusaders" out of Muslim lands; liberate Palestine, Afghanistan, Iraq; jihad against "near enemy" and "far enemy"; global Caliphate
Global Justice	UN conferences of 1990s; occasional support from EU and social democratic governments; PT government of Brazil; rise of other left-wing governments in Latin America	Third World Network; ENDA; Focus on the Global South; Oxfam; Jubilee 2000; World Social Forum	Against neoliberal globalization; for biodiversity and cultural diversity ("altermondialisation"); economic justice; end Third World debt; make poverty history; environmental protection; human rights; anti-war; "Another world is possible"

and heterogeneity, new forms of inequality and competition, and transnational forms of organizing and mobilizing.

2. What is called globalization-from-above is the latest stage of capital-ism on a world scale, involving the spread of neoliberal capitalism through investment, trade, and war.

3. Given the capitalist bases of globalization, the inequalities of class, gender, and race are maintained through processes of accumulation in the productive, reproductive, and virtual economies within and across the core, periphery, and semi-periphery of the world-system.[30]

4. Social movements—sustained contentious politics by mobilized groups that target states—have been affected by globalization in at least two ways: a) they are increasingly influenced by forces and fac-tors beyond national borders, and b) they have been expanding their scope above and across borders.

5. Transnational social movements are related to globalization in three ways: a) they are responses to the downside of globalization, specifi-cally, neoliberal capitalism; b) they reflect the global expansion of civil society, the transnational public sphere, and world culture; and (c) they benefit from opportunities and resources associated with the new computer and information technologies, notably the Internet.

6. Transnationalization is a deliberate strategy to increase the global reach of social movements and expand movement diversity, repre-sentation, and influence.

7. The transnational public sphere and global civil society are consti-tuted by social movements, advocacy networks, militant opposition groups, diverse publics, and media networks in contentious interac-tions and with different conceptions of "the good society." Not all participating networks, representations, and discourses, however, are emancipatory. It may be more useful, therefore, to refer to mul-tiple and sometimes overlapping transnational public spheres.

8. While social movement theory has emphasized the importance of organizations, the network form—with its flexibility and fluidity—appears to be most conducive to an era of globalization. The net-work structure is most characteristic of transnational social move-ments, including the three studied here.

9. Globalization presents the social sciences with analytical challenges: how to theorize the links between local and global, national and transnational; the capacity of states, social movements, and networks in a world of global capital; and the future of the world-system.

10. The study of social movements in a global era calls for an integrated framework drawing on world-system theory and world polity theory for a macrosociological and global perspective; employing feminism for an understanding of the gendered nature of institutions and movements; and invoking social movements concepts such as grievances, political opportunities, resources, mobilizing structures, and cultural frames. Such a holistic framework would help accomplish the goal of "globalizing social movement theory."[31]

ON STUDYING TRANSNATIONAL SOCIAL MOVEMENTS

As mentioned, globalization continues to present challenges for scholars of social change and for theory building. One issue pertains to the permanence of some of the new institutions and processes that are observed, including institutions of global governance and the rules of free trade. Is "globalization-from-above" a fait accompli or a transitional phase that can be supplanted by new social relations and forms of governance? What are the prospects of globalization's detractors? Are the responses known as "globalization-from-below" likely to be institutionalized? Answers to these questions require time and analysis. In the meantime, scholars continue to study globalization and transnational social movements. While the study of globalization includes poring over international data sets to discern patterns of economic and political governance, the study of transnational social movements requires a mix of methods, of which textual analysis, interviews, surveys, participant observation, and quantitative analysis are both important and typical.

Participant observation, surveys, in-depth interviews with key figures, close readings of network publications, analysis of websites, and the use of secondary sources are methods used by scholars of all three movements examined in this book. In studying Islamist movements, for example, scholars have visited offices, mosques, seminaries, and other institutions; conducted interviews (sometimes in prisons); utilized memoirs by former Islamists; and analyzed Islamist websites and publications. Reid and Chen used hyperlink and content analysis methodology to analyze extremist groups' websites.[32] Some have tracked the growth and visibility of militant groups through quantitative methods. The study of transnational feminist networks requires similar methods: attendance at feminist conferences; observation at protest events or UN conferences; reading of websites and publications; and interviews with key figures. With respect to analyses of the global justice movement (GJM), researchers have attended the World Social Forum, where they have conducted surveys and in-depth interviews; they have closely followed the writings and publications of scholar-activists and other GJM leaders; and they have quantified protests and events. The research products of the Institute for Research on World-Systems (IROWS), based at the University of California at Riverside, are especially helpful. Sociologist Christopher Chase-Dunn and his students have attended various World Social Forums, conducted surveys, and posted their findings on the IROWS website. The recent study on the GJM by sociologist Donatella della Porta and her associates is based on extensive and intensive observation of European movements and networks.

The present book is a work that synthesizes previous research, including my own. I have consulted the relevant secondary sources on globalization, social movements, and the global Islamist, feminist, and justice movements. In addition, I have examined movement websites and publications. The chapter on transnational feminist networks draws on my previous research but now also covers feminist activism against militarism and war. The explanatory framework establishes a relationship between "globalization-from-above" and "globalization-from-below"; shows how political processes, resources, networks, and framings are used by contenders to build their movements and advance their causes; identifies key features of Islamism, feminism, and global justice; and highlights the role of gender and masculinities.

This book is situated within critical globalization studies while also seeking to globalize social movement theorizing.[33] Conceptually, it establishes connections between globalization-from-above and globalization-from-below; politically it seeks to build a bridge between globalization studies and progressive global movements. This book is therefore intended for students, scholars, and activists alike.

CHAPTER 2

GLOBALIZATION AND COLLECTIVE ACTION

Globalization has been approached from different disciplinary vantage points, and debates have addressed such issues as whether globalization is at heart an economic or cultural process, the implications for state capacity, the social and gender impacts, and the effects of trade liberalization, direct foreign investment, and capital markets on growth, poverty, and inequality. The issue of periodization also has been debated: is globalization new or cyclical? My argument is that globalization is the latest stage of capitalism, and that its features have given rise to transnational movements of protest and resistance. Although capitalism has had other internationalizing stages, contemporary globalization has distinct features that enable forms of collective action rather broader in scale and scope than those that prevailed in the nineteenth or early twentieth centuries. And while the communist movement of the twentieth century was transnational and global in scope, it was more centralized than the transnational social movements found today. Gerlach's characterization of social movements as segmentary, polycentric, and reticulate is especially relevant to today's global movements. Collective action is organized at local, national, and transnational levels in fluid and flexible ways; it is directed at states, corporations, and institutions of global governance; and it calls for alternative values, institutions, and relations. With the global justice movement and transnational feminist networks, the means and strategies are deliberately non-violent. This is not the case, however, with militant Islamist movements.

This chapter provides an overview of discussions about globalization, considering its origins, dimensions, mechanisms, agents, and social implications. In addition, it examines the relationship between globalization and contemporary forms of collective action. Last but not least, we explore the status of the state in an era of globalization, and in relation to social movements, including transnational social movements.

FROM DEVELOPMENT TO GLOBALIZATION

Globalization became a buzzword in the mid-1990s, but before then scholars and activists had been focused on the development prospects of Third World countries and the damage that had been done by structural adjustment policies in the 1980s. Critiques of "the lost development decade"—which is what the 1980s era of Reganism, Thatcherism, and structural adjustments came to be known—intersected with earlier criticisms of the growing power of multinational corporations.[1] Meanwhile, veterans of Third World socialist or solidarity movements, left-wing groups, student movements, anti-Vietnam protests, and peace and anti-militarist causes—some of whom also were active in international development circles—networked at various conferences to exchange ideas and plan strategies.

The 1970s had been a time of both horror and hope. The 1973 coup d'état against the democratically elected socialist president of Chile, Dr. Salvadore Allende, ushered in both a reign of terror and the Global South's first experiment with a neoliberal economic policy framework. In her book *Shock Doctrine: The Rise of Disaster Capitalism*, Naomi Klein highlights this event as the harbinger of the more expansive scope of neoliberalism at century's end and into the new millennium.[2] At the same time, the 1975 defeat of the United States in Indochina and the unification of the Socialist Republic of Vietnam suggested a more hopeful era. The Cold War between the United States and the Soviet Union was in full swing, but the presence of a powerful communist bloc checked further aggression by the United States while also providing moral and financial support to various Third World movements and institutions.[3] The 1970s also saw the emergence of new international organizations supportive of Third World development, including the United Nations Conference on Trade and Development (UNCTAD), the South Center, and the Center on Transnational Corporations. The Society for International Development had been formed earlier but became an important forum for the discussion of development theories and strategies. What is more, the UN General Assembly issued a Declaration on the Establishment of a New International Economic Order, which targeted "the remaining vestiges of alien domination, colonialism, foreign occupation, racial discrimination, apartheid, and neo-colonialism." The declaration called for the "establishment of a just and equitable relationship" in the terms of trade between developed and developing countries; the "establishment of a new international monetary system" for the promotion of development in the Third World; and "securing favorable conditions for the transfer of financial resources to developing countries." It emphasized the need to "promote the transfer of technology and the creation of indigenous technology for the benefit of the developing countries in forms and in accordance with procedures which are suited to their economies," and the "necessity for all States to put an end to the waste of natural resources, including food products."[4] The NIEO would continue to inspire scholar-activists in Third World solidarity movements and development studies for at least ten years.

By the latter part of the 1980s, however, the NIEO had become a dead letter. Third World countries had borrowed heavily during the hopeful years of 1970s developmentalism. International banks were only too eager to lend, and the developing countries needed the loans to offset the effects of the oil price hikes of 1973 and 1979 as they continued to implement their development strategies.[5] When interest rates suddenly soared in 1980–1982, the Third World was plunged into what Cheryl Payer presciently had called "the debt trap."[6] The situation was exacerbated by the collapse of world market prices for Third World commodities such as copper, coffee, and oil. When developing countries turned to the World Bank and the International Monetary Fund (IMF) for new loans to service their debts, to carry out their development plans, or to guarantee their creditworthiness, the international financial institutions insisted on policy changes as a condition for additional loans. In the name of efficiency and balancing of budgets, the new "structural adjustment policies" called for austerity measures such as cuts in social spending, public sector restructuring, and the promotion of private capital. The immediate results, however, were perverse financial transfers from South to North as a result of debt servicing; deterioration of health, education, and welfare in many developing countries; falling real wages and incomes; a heavy household burden on women to compensate for income loss and social service cutbacks; and the collapse of governments and emergence of conflicts.

In concert with the World Bank and the IMF, the governments of Ronald Reagan in the United States and Margaret Thatcher in Great Britain became the proponents of the doctrine of neoliberal capitalism, which earlier had been implemented in Chile under the auspices of "the Chicago boys"—economist Milton Friedman and his associates from the University of Chicago. In the United States, neoliberal capitalism entailed deindustrialization and loss of job security; in the United Kingdom, it meant chipping away at the welfare state and undermining the trade unions. The shift from the post–World War II era of full employment and welfare-creation through government spending and industrial policy to the pre-eminence of big business and the operations of "the market" was now complete. The institutionalization of economic liberalism—free trade, free markets, and capitalist globalization—came to herald the end of "the global age of capitalism."[7] As the communist world weakened and then collapsed in the latter part of the 1980s, Prime Minister Thatcher's declaration that "there is no alternative" to global free-market capitalism seemed to ring true. Along with the U.S. government, the World Bank and the IMF became the prime agents of not only structural adjustment policies in the Third World but also the transformation of formerly socialist economies to capitalist economies in the 1990s. Meanwhile, dramatic reductions in transportation and communication costs combined with the breakdown of Fordist/Keynesian regimes in the core countries made it possible for firms to coordinate production on a truly global scale.[8]

GLOBALIZATION: THE LATEST STAGE OF CAPITALISM

On the left, scholars have analyzed these developments in at least two ways, with some emphasizing the role of class conflict and others stressing structural processes. David Harvey argues that neoliberalism, headed by the United States, has aimed for the restoration of class power to a small elite of financiers and corporate leaders, accomplished through forced privatization, or "accumulation by dispossession," as well as by the "virtual economy" of finance capital. William I. Robinson maintains that the reorganization of world production through new technologies and organizational innovations has given rise to a transnational capitalist class (TCC) and the making of a transnational state apparatus (TSA). For Harvey, globalization is "the new imperialism," while for Robinson it is a historic stage in the maturation of capitalism as a driving economic force.[9] Another structuralist position is taken by world-system theorists Immanuel Wallerstein and Christopher Chase-Dunn, who understand "globalization" as another word for the processes that they have always referred to as "world-systemic": integration into the economic zones of core, periphery, and semi-periphery, with their attendant hierarchies of states, and forms of resistance known as anti-systemic movements. Moreover, the capitalist world-economy has experienced cyclical processes and secular trends for hundreds of years, with various "waves of globalization."[10]

In fact, the two positions might not be so different. Globalization is certainly the result of forces such as technology, management innovations, and the market, but it does not just "happen." It is, rather, engineered and promoted by identifiable groups of people within identifiable organizations and states. Behzad Yaghmaian has argued that the emergence of the neoliberal model of capitalism is part of a systematic effort to lower the social value of labor power and provide the flexibility demanded for global accumulation by removing all national restrictions to the full mobility of capital and by imposing a restructuring of the labor market centered on the creation of flexible labor regimes.[11] Leslie Sklair, who like Robinson has theorized the making of a transnational capitalist class and state apparatus, adds to class theory by arguing that the TCC comprises not only those who own or control major corporations but also other groups whose resources and actions are deemed vital to the process of globalization: neoliberal bureaucrats and politicians, assorted professionals and technocrats, advertisers, and the mass media. These would be among the "globalizers," or those who have carefully promoted and disseminated the culture of consumer capitalism, as Sklair has demonstrated, or free market ideology, as discussed by Manfred Steger.[12] What is more, all agree that neoliberal global capitalism has produced social polarization—that is, widening inequalities and new categories of poor.

For progressives like Walden Bello, Martin Khor, David Korten, Jerry Mander, and others, globalization reproduces great and growing inequalities of wealth and incomes within and across countries. Furthermore, it is not an inevitable stage but the result of conscious neoliberal policy-making by "globalizers" (the agents of globalization), including multinational corporations and international financial institutions. In this view, globalization should be vigorously opposed by organized movements starting at the grassroots, local, and community levels.[13] Bello in particular has called for deglobalization. Many in the labor movement espouse a similar view. Trade union leaders have decried the social costs of globalization, such as unemployment, job insecurity, and continued poverty—the so-called race to the bottom—and they have called for the establishment of core labor standards, fair trade, democratization of global economic management, a tax on speculative financial flows (the so-called Tobin tax), and a shift of focus from markets to people.[14]

Global justice activists refer to growing worldwide inequalities as the reason for their anti-globalization stance, citing research by economists such as Angus Maddison, Anthony Atkinson, Lance Taylor, and Branko Milanovic as well as their own observations. Maddison's study of inequalities between nations since the nineteenth century shows rising cross-national inequalities since the 1970s, while Atkinson has documented rising inequalities in the industrialized countries (except in France). Taylor found that globalization and liberalization have not been uniformly favorable in terms of effects on growth and income distribution. Among the eighteen countries studied, only Chile after 1990 managed to combine high growth with decreasing inequality—in contrast to that country's increasing inequality over the preceding fifteen years.[15] In a recent book on measures of global inequality, Milanovic finds a complex situation including greater inequality within nations, greater differences between countries' mean incomes, and the "catching up" of large, poor countries such as India and China. Still, he finds that with adjustments for price levels (Purchasing Power Parity or PPP income), the bottom 90 percent of the world's population has half of world income, and the top 10 percent has the other half. In simple dollar terms (not adjusted for price levels), the top 10 percent has two-thirds of the world's income.[16]

Economists such as Joseph Stiglitz or Jeffrey Sachs, or those who produced the 1999 UNDP Human Development Report, see globalization as "Janus-faced" but with some capacity to reduce inequalities. In a report issued in April 2002, Oxfam–UK argued that trade liberalization could benefit developing countries, but it does not invariably do so. What is more, the multilateral trade system is weighted against the interests of developing countries mainly because core countries practice double standards by urging developing countries to liberalize while keeping their own markets closed to imports such as agricultural products and textiles. Policy recommendations, therefore, are that investment and trade between advanced and less developed countries should proceed equitably, and development assistance from North to South should increase.[17] (See table 2.1 for an elaboration of globalization's features, agents, and challengers.)

Another debate about globalization that is relevant to social movements concerns the extent to which the sovereignty of nation-states and the autonomy of national economies have been weakened. Some have argued that inasmuch as globalization entails "deterritorialization" through supra-national economic, political, and cultural processes and institutions, the nation-state as a power apparatus has been superseded. Capital flows and the growing power of institutions of global governance, such as

Table 2.1. Globalization: Features, Agents, and Challengers

	Features	Agents	Challengers
Economic	Neoliberal/free market capitalism; accumulation via investment, trade, aid	Multinational corporations, World Bank, IMF, WTO, OECD; the transnational capitalist class	Global justice movement
Political	Multilateralism, humanitarian operations	Intergovernmental organizations, transnational advocacy networks, international NGOs	*
	"Humanitarian intervention" and "preventive war"	NATO, United States, United Kingdom, Israel	Global justice movement, transnational feminist networks
Cultural	Consumer capitalism; free market ideology; electoral democracy	Multinational corporations, U.S. government, media	Global justice movement, Islamist movements
	Human rights, women's rights, environmental protection, human security, social justice, peace	Transnational feminist networks, global justice movement, civil society groups, UN agencies	*

*Occasionally, local non-state actors, authoritarian states, and U.S. preference for bilateralism or unilateralism.

the international financial institutions, leave states with greatly diminished options. In one version of this argument, Jessica Matthews has held that "the absolutes of the Westphalian system," including "territorially fixed states," are all dissolving. According to Susan Strange: "Where states were once the masters of markets, now it is the markets which, on many crucial issues, are the masters over the governments of states." In another version, fixed and strong state systems have been replaced by networks and flows. For Ulrich Beck, rather than the state as such: "We are living in an age of flows—flows of capital, cultural flows, flows of information and risks."[18] For Manuel Castells:

> Power . . . is no longer concentrated in institutions (the state), organizations (capitalist firms), or symbolic controllers (corporate media, churches). It is diffused in global networks of wealth, power, information, and images which circulate and transmute in a system of variable geometry and dematerialized geography. . . . The new power lies in the codes of information and in the images of representation around which societies organize their institutions, and people live their lives, and decide their behavior.[19]

Others do not go as far as Castells but argue that the activities of transnational corporations, global cities, and the transnational capitalist class render state-centered analysis outdated. Thus, Sklair's theory of the global system proposes taking the whole world as the starting point—that is, viewing the world not as an aggregate of nation-states but as a single unit and object of analysis. Sklair, William Robinson, and others have theorized the emergence of a deterritorialized transnational capitalist class, with its attendant institutions.[20] In contrast, Hirst and Thompson argue that the nation-state remains the dominant form of governance by comparison with more global or subnational levels. Similarly, Berger, Dore, and their collaborators show that national governments are still able to pursue different policies and maintain distinctive institutions, and they urge caution in generalizing about the extent of economic globalization.[21]

The debate on globalization and the state has implications for our study of globalization and social movements. As we saw in chapter 1, social movement theory posits a central role for the state in movement formation and evolution, captured in the wide-ranging concept "political opportunity structure." Sidney Tarrow defines social movements as mobilized groups engaged in sustained contentious interaction with power-holders in which at least one state is either a target or a participant.[22] What, then, do we make of a transnational social movement that targets institutions of global governance such as the World Bank, the International Monetary Fund, and the World Trade Organization? Does this reality mean that states have no effects on transnational movement prospects?

In fact, the state remains an important institution and the target of many social movement actions; particular states are often the targets of transnational protests. The state continues to matter for several reasons. First, neoliberal capitalism requires state regulation in order to function. As Tarak Barkawi observes, "States are not victims of economic globalization so much as they are *agents* of it."[23] Second, the state matters because international law confers obligations on states for the implementation of treaties, conventions, resolutions, and norms. The state also remains the body primarily responsible for guaranteeing the rights of citizens and human rights more broadly. For feminists, the state is the most relevant institution on matters of reproductive health and rights and of women's status in the family. True, the capacity of states to implement human rights may be compromised by poor resource endowments, by the power of foreign investors, or by foreign intervention, occupation, or conflict. There are states with the means and the capacity to provide civil, political, and social rights of citizenship, but which choose not to; instead, they repress any attempts at independent organizing or protest. Across the world-system's economic zones, we can see that state capacity is variable. This has implications not only for economic development but also for relations with civil society and social movements, and for movement prospects.

The presence or absence of elite allies and coalitions with state entities can be critical to a movement's formation and growth. In some cases, states have provided protest groups with needed leverage for their collective action. For example, the global justice movement found an ally in the Brazilian government. In particular, the Workers' Party and the city of Porto Alegre were crucial to the making of the World Social Forum.[24] In the past, Islamist movements received funding and moral support from the United States, Saudi Arabia, and other state entities. Thus, attention needs to be directed at sub- and supra-state processes, and the significance of processes of multilevel governance has to be recognized.

Nor has the concept of the nation-state disappeared. In the Middle East, proponents of Islamic fundamentalism and supporters of revolutionary Iranian Islam initially saw their movement as supra-national and railed against "artificial colonialist borders" that divided the *umma*, or the community of Muslim believers. But the activities and objectives of many political movements have largely remained within national borders. Territorial state nationalism has deep roots in the region, as the Iran–Iraq war of 1980–1988 and the overlong Israeli–Palestinian conflict have demonstrated all too vividly. Moreover, many Islamist groups have explicitly targeted what they have regarded as illegitimate state systems: the late Ayatollah Khomeini and his movement in Iran; the mujahideen in Afghanistan; the FIS in Algeria; Gama'a Islamiyya in Egypt. Indeed, research shows that many Islamist movements are focused on national-level problems and have national-level goals even while they may be in close contact with other Islamist movements and governments (for example, Palestinian Hamas and Lebanese Hezbollah). However, the emergence of Osama bin Laden's al-Qaeda network in the late 1990s would seem to suggest that globalization facilitates the formation of loosely organized, deterritorialized transnational groups. Thus far, as the latest stage of capitalism, globalization has not supplanted the international system of states even though it has generated powerful new global institutions and engendered protest movements on a world scale. We may tentatively conclude that globalization provides a new opportunity structure for social movements—one that enables them to take on a transnational form with a global reach.

Economists and world-system sociologists view globalization in largely economic terms, but for many observers it is a multifaceted phenomenon. It refers, inter alia, to time-space compression, world culture, the increase in the available modes of organization, the emergence of multiple and overlapping identities, and the arising of hybrid sites such as world cities, free trade zones, offshore banking facilities, border zones, and ethnic mélange neighborhoods. Jan Aart Scholte discusses globalization as deterritorialization, producing and diffusing "supraterritorial," "transworld," and "transborder" relations between people. He and Jan Nederveen Pieterse regard "hybridization" to be an important facet of globalization, although both also highlight the unevenness, asymmetry, and inequality that are embedded in the new global mélange.[25] These observations have implications for social movements and transnational networks. Among other things, these aspects of globalization permit interactions, connections, and mobilizations conducive to transnational collective action. (See figure 2.1.)

The various aspects of globalization have promoted growing contacts between different cultures, leading partly to greater understanding and cooperation and partly to the emergence of transnational communities and hybrid identities. But globalization also has hardened the opposition of different identities. This is one way of understanding the emergence of reactive movements such as fundamentalism and communalism, which seek to recuperate

Global Opportunity Structure
- Intergovernmental and governance structure
- Elite allies at international level
- International law
- Computer technologies

Cross-border Mobilizations
- Use of organizational infrastructure
- New networks, cells, associations
- Recruitment and financial drives

Cross-cultural Framings
- Shared identities
- Moral outrage
- Acceptance of tactics
- Website activism

Global Social Movement

Figure 2.1. The Making of a Global Social Movement

traditional patterns, including patriarchal gender relations, in reaction to the "westernizing" trends of globalization. Various forms of identity politics are the paradoxical outgrowth of globalization, which Benjamin Barber aptly summarizes as "jihad vs. McWorld."[26] He uses the term "jihad" as shorthand to describe religious fundamentalism, disintegrative tribalism, ethnic nationalisms, and similar kinds of identity politics carried out by local peoples "to sustain solidarity and tradition against the nation-state's legalistic and pluralistic abstractions as well as against the new commercial imperialism of McWorld."[27] Jihad is in struggle against modernity and cultural imperialism alike, and "answers the complaints of those mired in poverty and despair as a result of unregulated global markets and of capitalism uprooted from the humanizing constraints of the democratic nation-state."[28]

GLOBALIZATION, EMPIRE, AND HEGEMONIC MASCULINITIES

Jihad is also in struggle against Empire.[29] In particular, many Islamist groups look beyond the "near enemy" (their own rulers or states) and target the hegemonic behavior of the United States (the "far enemy"), even though they were once supported by the United States. In world-historical terms, the U.S.–supported war in Afghanistan in the 1980s was especially significant. Its outcomes entailed the collapse of the Soviet Union and world communism; the expansion of a militarized Islamist movement; and the emergence of a unipolar world led by the United States.[30]

Although the United States had been the world-system's hegemon since the 1950s, its power had been checked frequently by the Soviet Union. The end of the Cold War and the collapse of the Soviet Union left the United States in a position of unparalleled military predominance. In the 1990s the U.S. ruling elite began using this strategic asset to redraw the imperial map of the world, first in the Gulf War and then in the Kosovo war. It should be noted that this development encompassed the administrations of the first President Bush and of President Bill Clinton, with the cooperation of both political parties. The new imperial design did not become fully realized, however, until the rise of the neoconservative wing of the ruling elite and the victory of George W. Bush in the presidential election of 2000. Even then, this scheme awaited the conditions in which it could be implemented. The attack on the World Trade Center in 2001 created those conditions.

For a while, following the invasion of Afghanistan in late 2001 and the routing of the Taliban, it appeared that the neoconservative "Project for the New American Century" was being successfully implemented. However, the invasion of Iraq in 2003 served to underline the limits of U.S. power. These limits have at least three sources. First, there is the relative economic weakness of the United States. Unlike during the "golden age" following World War II, the rise of other advanced economies and the strength of the euro make the world-system a much more competitive environment. The combination of relative economic decline and overwhelming military strength propelled the Bush administration to rely on its military capacity to discipline both its allies and its competitors on the world stage. Second, the limits of U.S. power are seen in recent factionalism within the ruling elite, particularly in the disagreements between the Democrats and the Republicans over the conduct, costs, and morality of the war in Iraq (and the war in Afghanistan).[31] Third, there is the concerted resistance to the U.S. government's designs in Iraq—invasion, occupation, and privatization of the country's resources and of the security apparatus.[32] The resistance is both homegrown and transnational, and it has been fierce. It consists of nationalists but largely of Islamists with sophisticated weapons, a transnational reach, and patriarchal agendas.

Here we must pause to take into account competing hegemonic masculinities, such as those of al-Qaeda and of the Bush administration. Hegemonic masculinity has become a key concept in gender analysis since R. W. Connell identified it as a particular culture's standards and ideal of real manhood, at a particular time in history.[33] In countries such as the United States and Australia, hegemonic masculinity is defined by physical strength and bravado, exclusive heterosexuality, suppression of "vulnerable" emotions such as remorse and uncertainty, economic independence, authority over women and other men, and intense interest in sexual "conquest." What Connell has defined as "emphasized femininity" is constructed around adaptation to male power. Its central feature is attractiveness to men, which includes physical appearance, ego massaging, suppression of "power" emotions such as anger, nurturance of children, exclusive heterosexuality, sexual availability without sexual assertiveness, and sociability. Both standards and ideals may be observed in many cultures, albeit with variations on the sexual element.[34] Hegemonic masculinity, in particular, is reproduced in various social institutions, including the media, the sports arena, the family, the military, and sometimes in religious institutions. In turn, it can be expressed at the level of an individual or a collective: a frat house, a military unit, a street gang, a movement, a political regime.

A similar analysis is put forth by Lauren Langman and Douglas Morris, in their discussion of "heroic masculinities."[35] As they point out, civilizations and cultures based on conquest or expansion, societies where politics and militarism are fused, and countries where the military is a central and valorized institution all exhibit discourses, images, and practices of heroic masculinity. In considering American society and the role of its military in both economic growth and empire building, and in considering the foundational narratives of heroic masculinity in Islam, one can easily imagine a "clash of heroic masculinities" (as Langman and Morris put it) between the American security state and a transnational Islamist network such as al-Qaeda. From a feminist perspective, hegemonic or heroic masculinity is a causal factor in war, as well as in women's oppression. As Anne Sisson Runyan has aptly noted, "The world is awash with contending masculinities that vie to reduce women to symbols of either fundamentalism or Western hypermodernity."[36]

In a way, contemporary rivalries in hegemonic or heroic masculinity mirror the inter-capitalist rivalries of the early part of the twentieth century—which led to World War I and World World II. They underlie many of the factors that have been attributed to the "new conflicts" of the post–Cold War era, such as the emergence of a global weapons market, the decreasing capacity of states to uphold the monopoly of violence, inter-ethnic competition, and Barber's "jihad vs. McWorld."[37] Indeed, rival masculinities constitute a key factor in the conflicts that emerge over natural resources, such as oil or diamonds; in aggressive nationalism and ethnic rivalries; and in politicized religious projects. Hegemonic masculinity is a central ideological pillar of both Empire and some forms of resistance, notably militant Islam.

ON GLOBAL SOCIAL MOVEMENTS AND TRANSNATIONAL COLLECTIVE ACTION

The capitalist world-system has often produced anti-systemic movements that cross borders and boundaries, while national-level class conflicts and political contradictions similarly have generated forms of collective action and social protest, including social movements. For example, sociologists Susan Eckstein and Timothy Wickham-Crowley identified several arenas of rights that were at risk in Latin America as a result of the spread of neoliberal economic policies, and categorized the relevant social movements that emerged: protests against cuts in urban services; strikes and labor struggles; gender-based movements; and rural movements.[38] Some of these movements have come to be connected to the global justice movement or to global feminism. In turn, the global feminist, Islamist, and justice movements are part of the world-system, are products of globalization, and target both states and the global order. They also reflect the growth of what has been called global civil society and the transnational public sphere.

The UN conferences of the 1990s were important to the making of global civil society and the growth of transnational social movements and their organizations/networks: the UN Conference on Environment and Development (UNCED), held in Rio de Janeiro in June 1992; the World Conference on Human Rights, held in Vienna in June 1993; the International Conference on Population and Development (ICPD), held in Cairo in September 1994; the World Summit on Social Development, held in Copenhagen in March 1995; and the Fourth World Conference on Women, held in Beijing in September 1995. As more and more governments signed on to the international treaties associated with these and related conferences, their agreements created a conducive global opportunity structure for social movements and civil society actors. State integration into the world polity enabled cross-border networking and mobilizations, and facilitated cross-cultural framings.

In recent years many scholars have begun to focus on global or transnational social movements, while others have analyzed transnational advocacy networks. If a social movement is "a sustained campaign of claims-making, using repeated performances that advertise the claim, based on organizations, networks, traditions, and solidarities that sustain these activities," then transnational social movements are "socially mobilized groups with constituents in at least two states, engaged in sustained contentious interactions with power-holders in at least one state other than their own, or against an international institution, or a multinational economic actor."[39] As discussed in chapter 1, transnational social movements often are comprised of domestically based or transnational networks, including transnational advocacy networks.

What makes transnational activists different from domestic activists is their ability to shift their activities among levels and across borders, coordinating with groups outside their own country. As has been widely discussed in the literature, this has been made possible by one of the "gifts" of globalization—the new information and computer technologies, mobile phones and, to a lesser extent, satellite television. The Internet, in particular, has allowed for rapid communication and coordination; Internet-savvy transnational networks have set up extensive, interactive, and increasingly sophisticated multimedia websites, where one can find statements, research reports, and manifestoes, as well as discussion forums, chat rooms, tutorials, and digital libraries.[40] Such websites, many of which are linked to each other, create or support communities of activists while also providing them with resources.

Some scholars have tried to empirically test the relationship between globalization—whether measured by growing inequalities or by state integration in the world polity—and the rise and spread of global contentious politics and of transnational social movements. Jackie Smith and Dawn Wiest, for example, have analyzed the impact of world culture and world polity on the spread of progressive, non-violent social movements. They have found a positive relationship between state integration into world polity and civil society integration into transnational networks or global civil society. Others have looked at the relationship between economic globalization or world culture and less salutary forms of global contentious politics, including violent militancy.[41] In much the same way that globalization itself is complex and contradictory, the transnational social movements associated with it or resulting from it are also complex and contradictory. That is, globalization has produced life-affirming non-violent social movements but also deadly rebellions, martyrdom operations, and transnational networks of violent extremists.

What is it that transnational social movements do? Chadwick Alger's observation of a decade ago remains apt, at least with respect to the non-violent transnational movements: they create and activate global networks to mobilize pressure outside states; they participate in multilateral and inter-governmental political arenas; they act and agitate within states; and they enhance public awareness and participation.[42] Time and space compression through the Internet has made all this easier to accomplish. Thus activists are able to organize structures above the national level uniting adherents across borders with similar identities and goals around a common agenda. In the process, they contribute to the making of global civil society or a transnational public sphere. As Guidry, Kennedy, and Zald have noted: "Globalization has in fact brought social movements together across borders in a 'transnational public sphere,' a real as well as conceptual space in which movement organizations interact, contest each other, and learn from each other."[43]

In their study of the global justice movement, Pianta and Marchetti highlight the link between global civil society and global social movements. Global civil society is "the sphere of cross-border relationships and activities carried out by collective actors—social movements, networks, and civil society organizations—that are independent from governments and private firms and operate outside the international reach of states and markets." Global social movements are "cross-border, sustained, and collective social mobilizations on global issues, based on permanent and/or occasional groups, networks, and campaigns with a transnational organizational dimension moving from shared values and identities that challenge and protest economic or political power and campaign for change in global issues. They share a global frame of the problems to be addressed, have a global scope of action, and might target supranational or national targets."[44]

Are all transnational movements actors within global civil society? Here we must draw attention to the normative dimension of certain social science concepts and categories. Many scholars have viewed social movements and civil society (as well as revolutions and liberation movements) through a progressive lens. Mary Kaldor has noted that civil society tends to be defined as "the medium through which one or many social contracts between individuals, both women and men, and the political and economic centers of power are negotiated and reproduced." This is a "rights-based definition of civil society . . . about politics from below and about the possibility for human emancipation."[45] However, the rise of non-state and anti-corporate movements, organizations, and networks that appear to eschew values of equality, democracy, and human rights has called such a view into question. Are all non-state actors that engage in negotiated interactions with state actors, whether at the local or global levels, constituent elements of civil society? What of a network such as al-Qaeda? Or the cells created by disaffected young Muslim men in Europe that planned and executed terrorist bombings? Or neo-Nazi groups in Europe? Kaldor concedes that some of the most vital forms of global civil society to emerge are found in religious and nationalist social movements, many of which are profoundly anti-democratic, and that this has tempered the initial enthusiasm for civil society among many activists. To avoid subjectivity, she and the other editors of the *Global Civil Society Yearbook* have stated: "We believe that the normative content is too contested to be able to form the basis for any operationalization of the concept."[46]

Conversely, Rupert Taylor takes a strong position in favor of the normative content, and offers a subjective as well as objective analysis of global civil society. There is little to be gained analytically, he argues, in including any and all non-state actors in the definition of (global) civil society. This is also the position of the transnational feminist network Women Living Under Muslim Laws, which has issued statements decrying women's human rights violations by non-state actors and has published a manual on the subject.[47] Taylor maintains that "at an objective level, global civil society structurally relates to a multi-organizational field that encompasses both those organizations that tend to work within the INGO and nation-state system, follow professionalized advocacy styles and agendas, and are involved in complex multilateralism, *and* those movements—anti-neoliberal and anti-corporate alike—committed to street protest and other forms of direct action." At a subjective level, he continues, "the intent of global civil society activism is to confront neoliberal globalization and create a better world through advocating a fairer, freer, and more just global order." Global civil society, then, should be taken to be "a complex multi-organizational field that explicitly excludes reactionary—racist, fascist, or fundamentalist—organizations and movements."[48]

Viewed in normative terms, therefore, global civil society is the site of democratic, non-violent, and emancipatory associational interaction. Viewed in a strictly empirical way, however, (global) civil society is not a necessarily emancipatory sphere of action and identity, and not all (global) social movements are progressive. Certainly, the SPR nature of social movements guarantees the presence of different tendencies within a movement, including radical, militant, or even terrorist wings. Thus we can distinguish between progressive and reactionary social movements and civil society actors. Progressive social movements and civil society actors seek to negotiate new relationships and arrangements with states and with institutions of global governance through popular support and respect for human rights. Terrorist factions do not work to cultivate popular support; nor do they respect human rights. This book, therefore, recognizes that globalization has led to the formation of all manner of non-state organizing and collective action. Not all, however, may be viewed as emancipatory or transformative.

All transnational collective action takes place within, and is shaped by, the capitalist world-system and its current phase of globalization. In turn, globalization has given rise to criticisms and grievances, as well as opportunities for collective action. It has created a global opportunity structure and enabled cross-border framings and mobilizations. These framings and mobilizations may be driven by proximate causes but, as was discussed in chapter 1, are rooted in pre-existing discourses, collective memories, and organizational infrastructures. Islamist activism has been motivated by corrupt, authoritarian, or pro-Western regimes in their own Muslim-majority countries; by solidarity with their confrères in Palestine, Iraq, and Afghanistan; and by opposition to secularizing and westernizing tendencies. The transnational Islamist movement consists of groups and networks ranging from moderate to extremist, using methods that range from parliamentarism to spectacular violence. Transnational feminist activism is motivated by concern for women's human rights in an era of neoliberal globalization, militarism, war, and patriarchal fundamentalisms. Transnational feminist networks—the principal mobilizing structure of global feminism—consist of women from three or more countries who mobilize for research, lobbying, advocacy, and civil disobedience to protest gender injustice and promote women's human rights, equality, and peace. The global justice movement consists of loosely organized mobilized groups that protest the downside of globalization and call for economic and social justice. A key institution is the World Social Forum (WSF), a gathering place for the numerous transnational networks and nationally based advocacy groups that have grown exponentially since the mid-1990s. Initially organized by the Brazilian Workers' Party and the landless peasant movement, the WSF was intended to be a forum for the participants and supporters of grassroots movements across the globe, and a counterpart to forums of representatives of governments, political parties, and corporations.

The three movements examined in this book are interconnected, inasmuch as feminists and moderate Islamists have taken part in the WSF; and the global justice movement includes individuals and groups active in transnational feminist networks. All three movements are counter-hegemonic in that they are opposed to globalization's hegemonic tendencies of neoliberalism, expansion, and war. Each movement itself is transnational, inasmuch as it targets states and international institutions, and is a coalition of local, grassroots groups as well as trans-border groups. But the three differ in significant ways. For Islamists, the solution to current problems is the widespread application of Islamic laws and norms; global justice activists present a variety of alternatives to neoliberalism, from de-globalization to cosmopolitan social democracy; transnational feminists insist on the application of international conventions on women's human rights. The similarities and differences, as well as the connections to globalization, will be elucidated in the subsequent chapters.

CONCLUSION

Globalization remains a contested subject for scholars, policy-makers, and activists. Its enthusiasts try to show the promises of free trade, deregulation, and flexibility while its detractors emphasize the problems of inequalities, unfair trade relations, political domination, and militarism. Meanwhile, many organized groups and networks—some associated with Islamism and others with the global justice movement, including feminist networks—have taken a stance against the adverse effects of globalization.

Globalization has created both grievances that motivate protest and opportunities for mobilization. The contemporary era of globalization is marked by a distinct set of economic policies, the worldwide dissemination of cultural products, and a political-military project of domination. It has engendered competition and contestation—even among its main agents and supporters—and grievances and resistance from its detractors. Among its detractors are transnational activists who promote an alternative kind of globalization.

This chapter has shown that a key characteristic of the era of late capitalism, or globalization, is the proliferation of networks of activists within transnational social movements. Guidry, Kennedy, and Zald have correctly regarded globalization as a new opportunity structure for social movements.

Globalization brings important new resources to mobilization efforts, and movements can frame their claims in terms that resonate beyond territorial borders. We have noted the paradoxes of globalization: while its economic, political-military, and cultural aspects have engendered grievances and opposition, it also has provided the means for rapid cross-border communication, coordination, mobilization, and action. The next chapters explore in more detail how movements of Islamists, feminists, and global justice activists address globalization.

CHAPTER 3

ISLAMIST MOVEMENTS

Like the women's movement and the global justice movement (see chapters 4 and 5), Islamism may be seen as a "movement of movements." Its overarching common goal is the establishment or reinforcement of Islamic laws and norms as the solution to economic, political, and cultural crises. And yet Islamist movements are heterogeneous and diverse, evincing different tactics and strategies in achieving their goals. This structural feature is in keeping with the SPR character of social movements, as discussed in the previous chapter. Distinctions have been made between "moderate" and "extremist" Islamists. Generally, moderates engage in non-violent organizing and advocacy in civil society. They form or join political parties and field candidates in parliamentary elections, even though they may be critical of existing political arrangements. Such groups include the Muslim Brotherhood of Egypt and Jordan, Islah of Yemen, the Justice and Development Party (AKP) of Turkey, and the Parti de la Justice et du Développement of

Morocco (PJD). Extremists, on the other hand, call for the violent over-throw of political systems they regard as anti-Islamic, westernized, and dic-tatorial. They operate clandestinely, form networks and cells across coun-tries, and may engage in spectacular forms of violence. They brand as un-Islamic any participation in electoral politics. Also known as salafists or jihadists (or salafi jihadists), they may or may not have links to the transna-tional network of al-Qaeda, with its satellites in south Asia, North Africa, and Iraq. In between the polar opposites are groups that could be called rad-ical Islamists, inasmuch as they call for Islamization of their societies and often engage in fiery rhetoric (for example, calling for executions of apos-tates or infidels, jihad against oppressors, and so on) but may not them-selves engage in violent acts. Such groups include Wahhabists influenced by Saudi Arabia, such as the United Kingdom–based Islamist groups Tablighi Jamaat and Hizb ut-Tahrir. (See table 3.1.)

Islamist groups have been studied by scholars including Olivier Roy, Gilles Kepel, Fawaz Gerges, Mohammed Hafez, and Quintan Wiktorowicz. Their studies elucidate the common discourses but also the divergent strate-gies deployed by Islamists, as well as the factors that drive Islamist action. Political scientist Fawaz Gerges conducted interviews with scores of ji-hadists during 1999 and 2000. He stresses the importance of distinguishing between national jihad and transnational jihad, arguing that the latter arose from the failure of the former. Some national jihadists and other Islamists have condemned the indiscriminate violence of global jihadists such as al-Qaeda. Sociologist Quintan Wiktorowicz's study of reformist and militant salafi Islam shows how salafi networks and organizations developed, changed, and helped drive political crises from Algeria to Afghanistan over the past three decades. Jordan's salafists, he demonstrates, now focus on spreading their ideas through study circles and publishing. He asserts that "radicals respond rationally and strategically to structures of opportunity." And he agrees with Mohammed Hafez, who has argued that Islamic radicals turn to violence when the state forecloses opportunities for participation and inclusion in the public sphere and resorts to repression.[1]

The Islamist groups mentioned above should be distinguished sharply from a tendency that some scholars call liberal or democratic Islam. One scholar and proponent of liberal Islam was the late Pakistani scholar Fazlur Rahman.[2] In the Islamic Republic of Iran, a generation of lay advocates and dissident clerics known as "the new religious intellectuals" emerged in the 1990s, calling for human rights and civil liberties informed by an emanci-patory interpretation of Islam, along with the separation of the clerical es-tablishment and religious law from the state apparatus.[3] Another version of

Table 3.1. Types of Islamist or Muslim Movements and Organizations, 1980s–Present

	Parliamentary	Liberal/Democratic	Radical	Jihadist
Afghanistan				Mujahideen; Taliban
Algeria			FIS	GIA
Egypt	Muslim Brotherhood			Islamic Jihad; Gama'a Islamiyya
Indonesia				Jemaah Islamiah*
Islamic Republic of Iran		"New Religious Intellectuals"		
Jordan	Muslim Brotherhood/ Islamic Action Front			Salifiyya movement; Jaish Muhammad
Lebanon	Hezbollah		Hezbollah	
Morocco	PJD (Justice and Development Party)			Fatah al-Islam**
Pakistan	Jamaat-i Islam		Jamaat-i Islam	
Malaysia	PAS	Sisters in Islam	PAS	
Palestine	Hamas		Hamas	Islamic Jihad; Fatah al-Islam
Tunisia	An-Nahda/MDS			
Turkey	AKP (Justice and Development Party)	AKP		
United Kingdom			Tablighi Jamaat, Hizb ut-Tahrir	Al-Muhajiroun
Global				Al-Qaeda

*Responsible for 2002 bombings in Bali and Jakarta; **responsible for summer 2007 uprising in Palestinian camps.

liberal and democratic Islam is found in the global network of Islamic feminists, who have taken issue with patriarchal and violent interpretations of Islam, seek legal reforms, and call for women's rights through their own re-readings of the Quran and early Islamic history. Among the most organized, vocal, and visible are Malaysia's Sisters in Islam (SIS), who work with feminist groups across the globe and are associated with the transnational feminist network Women Living Under Muslim Laws. In the United States, a number of such liberal Muslim groups and institutions exist, including Muslim Wake-Up, the Free Muslims, Asma Society, and the Center for the Study of Islam and Democracy, based in Washington, D.C. Internationally, the Swiss-born intellectual Tariq Ramadan is known as a proponent of non-violent and liberal Islam, although some feminist groups continue to view him with suspicion.[4]

This chapter will examine the origins, activities, and discourses of Islamist movements, highlighting their relationship to globalization processes and drawing attention to similarities and differences with other transnational social movements. But first, how might we define Islamism? Wiktorowicz prefers the term "Islamic activism," which he defines as "the mobilization of contention to support Muslim causes." His definition would include both Islamic fundamentalism and political Islam, whether in their moderate or radical tendencies. Wiktorowicz maintains that "Islamists are Muslims who feel compelled to act on the belief that Islam demands social and political activism, either to establish an Islamic state, to proselytize to reinvigorate the faithful, or to create a separate union for Muslim communities." He argues, as does Mohammed Hafez, that Islamist rebellions arise from state repression.[5]

A rather less sympathetic definition of Islamism is provided by the Syrian political philosopher Sadik Al-Azm:

> Islamism is a highly militant mobilizing ideology selectively developed out of Islam's scriptures, texts, legends, historical precedents, organizations, and present-day grievances, all as a defensive reaction against the long-term erosion of Islam's primacy over the public, institutional, economic, social, and cultural life of Muslim societies in the twentieth century. The ideology is put in practice by resurrecting the early concept of Islamic jihad in its most violent and aggressive forms against an environing world of paganism, polytheism, idolatry, godlessness, infidelity, atheism, apostasy, and unbelief known to that ideology as the Jahiliyya of the twentieth century.[6]

Similarly, Egyptian political economist Samir Amin, a key figure in the global justice movement and a long-time activist in Third World, anti-imperialist, and socialist movements, has penned harsh criticisms of Islamism, including a recent essay entitled "Political Islam in the Service of Imperialism." He maintains that Islamist movements should be understood as politically and culturally right-wing, pointing out that the Muslim Brotherhood members of the Egyptian parliament "reinforce[d] the rights of property owners to the detriment of the rights of tenant farmers (the majority of the small peasantry)."[7]

As will become evident in this chapter, my understanding of Islamism combines elements of all three perspectives but moves beyond them, too. Like Wiktorowicz and Hafez, I believe that the concepts and categories of social movement theory can be applied to elucidate the dynamics of Islamist activism. However, I do not believe that Islamists are motivated exclusively by state repression; as discussed in chapters 1 and 2, social-psychological explanations, including the role of masculine identities and religiously informed "heroic masculinities," are pertinent. The violence perpetrated over Salman Rushdie's book *The Satanic Verses* in 1989 and over the Danish cartoons caricaturing Prophet Muhammad in 2006 was not related to state repression. Here my approach to Islamist politics is similar to that of Amin, and my definition of Islamism is more consistent with that of Al-Azm: a militantly politicized movement, network, or ideology selectively based on Islamic theology and history but motivated by contemporary developments. My analysis, however, situates the rise and expansion of contemporary Islamism in world-systemic and globalization processes while also recognizing the gendered nature of Islamist politics and practices. And in this book, the juxtaposition of Islamism with transnational feminism and the global justice movement reveals stark differences in their frames and strategies.

ORIGINS OF ISLAMIST MOVEMENTS

Contemporary Islamist movements have their origins in the history and theology of Islam, and this is also part of their own ideological frames. Salafists and jihadists in particular emphasize the doctrinal obligation of Muslims to defend the faith when Islam is deemed to be under threat. They point out that the Prophet Muhammad and his companions engaged in battle to defend themselves and spread the faith, and they interpret Quranic verses in particular ways to justify attacks on "apostates" and "infidels."[8] In contrast, moderate and liberal Muslims emphasize the "inner struggle" that Muslims are called on to perform, in order to strengthen their faith. Applying a historical perspective, they note that in early Islam, apostasy was equivalent to the modern concept of treason; hence in an era of modern nation-states, changing one's religion cannot be considered a treasonous, capital offense.

As noted in chapter 1, many contemporary Islamists have been inspired by the writings of Islamic intellectuals such as Egypt's Rashid Rida, Hassan al-Banna, and Sayyid Qutb, and Iran's Ayatollah Khomeini. Certainly these texts provide a theological and intellectual context for Islamism. And yet, national and global political factors constitute critical determinants of political Islam. The Cold War and the fervent anti-communism of the United States led to sustained efforts to eliminate left-wing movements and governments, as well as nationalist governments perceived to be soft on communism. Seminal events would include the 1953 coup d'état against Iran's Prime Minister Mossadegh; the 1965 coup in Indonesia that eliminated the Communist Party and brought the military dictator Suharto to power; the support for military dictatorships in Pakistan and Bangladesh in the 1980s; and the support for Islamist rebels fighting a left-wing government in Afghanistan in the 1980s. Throughout this period, the United States was in close alliance with Saudi Arabia, an oil-rich country that guaranteed the flow of oil to the West, used its wealth to help build Muslim institutions and networks across the globe, and participated in the fight against communism.[9]

Many Muslim intellectuals and clerical leaders had long been opposed to the secularism of communist movements. The growth of left-wing movements in the 1960s and 1970s led many regimes to encourage the Islamic tide in hopes of neutralizing the left. This was the basic strategy of President Anwar Sadat, who released the Muslim Brothers from prison in an attempt to counter the Egyptian left in his campaign of de-Nasserization. Iran's Shah Mohammad Reza Pahlavi followed the same strategy in the early 1970s, as did Turkish authorities after the 1980 military coup. Indeed, in the latter case, as the generals' overriding objective was to rid Turkish society of Marxist ideology and parties, they encouraged Islamic ideas and education as an antidote. Thus, in 1982 the military regime made the teaching of Islam compulsory in schools; since 1967 it had been optional. When Islamists in Iran were able to seize control of the 1978–1979 revolution, the victory of the "Islamic revolution" inspired and encouraged Muslims and Islamists throughout the world.[10] In 1981 Egyptian Islamists assassinated president Anwar Sadat. In 1992, the U.S.-supported Afghan mujahideen toppled the modernizing government of president Najibullah. By this time, Islamist networks existed across the globe, and they steadily proliferated. The collapse of the Soviet Union may have been celebrated by some, notably the conservative political theorist Francis Fukuyama, as the harbinger of the worldwide expansion of liberal democracy. But in the Muslim world it meant the end of the reigning alternative ideology of socialism/communism. In his study of the "unholy wars," John Cooley refers to the "strange love affair which went disastrously wrong: the alliance, during the second half of the twentieth century, between the United States of America and some of the most conservative and fanatical followers of Islam."[11]

Meanwhile, the global and epochal shift from Keynesianism to neoliberalism—along with the end of the Third World, the non-aligned movement, and emergent discussion of a new international economic order—created economic conditions that would generate grievances, protests, and mobilizations. The shift in political economy from state-directed development to privatization was accompanied by political liberalization, which occurred in some measure in countries such as Turkey, Egypt, Jordan, and Algeria. This broad world-systemic perspective is critical to an understanding of Islamist movements, because it contextualizes the protests that arose over structural adjustments and unemployment; the spread of Islamic NGOs and their social welfare activities; and the political openings that allowed the "Islamic alternative" to present itself, in some cases as moderate and parliamentarian and in other as radical and jihadist.

Our analysis is not complete, however, without reference to sociodemographics and social psychology, including issues of urbanization, anomie, and class background. As early research by Saad Eddin Ibrahim and by John Entelis revealed, the recruits of Islamist movements were often first-generation urbanites from the lower middle classes and conservative family backgrounds. Such socio-demographic features are widely theorized to evince status anxiety and cultural discomfort.[12] This pattern suggested parallels with recruits to right-wing or fascistic movements.[13] At the same time, feminist research showed that women's growing social visibility and participation was challenging men's dominance in public spaces, rendering recent migrants and men of the lower middle class and conservative background alienated and angry. These conditions made such men highly vulnerable to an ideology whose grievances and solutions resonated because it was anchored in religion.[14] In the case of Islamic fundamentalism and political Islam, therefore, a linkage between structural strain and movement contention at a national level could plausibly be made. In turn, global processes of which Muslim societies were a part exacerbated structural strain. Whether in Europe or in Muslim-majority countries, the Islamist message came to resonate largely with young men confronting socio-economic difficulties and cultural changes that provoked feelings of anxiety, alienation, and anger. Islam became the source of a mobilizing ideology and of organizational resources used to combat domestic injustices, cultural imperialism, and changes to traditional notions of the family.

To summarize the argument, I present a set of propositions regarding the causes and characteristics of Islamist movements.[15]

- Islamist movements emerged in the context of the worldwide shift from Keynesianism to neoliberalism. Rising indebtedness, unemployment, and problems arising from austerity measures and economic restructuring in the 1980s added to tensions everywhere. These were linked to global restructuring and recession, or what world-system theorists refer to as the B-phase downturn of the Kondratieff wave; the falling price of oil on the world market had an adverse effect on development and on living standards.
- Politically, many Muslim-majority countries were characterized by authoritarian and neopatriarchal state systems that silenced left-wing and liberal forces while fostering religious institutions in their search for legitimacy. This created an ideological and political gap that could be filled by Islamist groups with substantial resources and a culturally resonant frame.
- Islamist movements also arose in the context of the demographic transition, the result of which was accelerated population growth and a social burden of a larger, more youthful, and more dependent population in Muslim-majority countries. Many young men found themselves without secure prospects, and became willing recruits to Islamism.
- In many parts of the Muslim world, capitalist and precapitalist modes of production coexisted, with corresponding social and ideological forms as well as types of consciousness. There was an uneasy coexistence of modern and traditional social classes, such as the Westernized upper middle class on the one hand and the traditional petty bourgeoisie organized around the bazaar and the mosque on the other. The urban centers all had large numbers of people outside the formal wage market and among the ranks of the urban poor and uneducated.
- Female education and employment, while still limited, had been increasing, thanks to economic development and the expanding state apparatus. This trend challenged and slowly weakened the system of

patriarchal gender relations, creating status inconsistency and anxiety on the part of the men of the petty bourgeoisie. Changes in gender relations, the structure of the family, and the position of women resulted in contestation between modern and traditional social groups over the nature and direction of cultural institutions and legal frameworks. A kind of gender conflict emerged, although this conflict had class dimensions as well.

- The non-resolution of the Israeli–Palestinian problem and a pervasive sense of injustice caused by Israeli and American actions helped to engender Islamist movements. The failure of the secular-democratic project of the PLO encouraged the Islamist alternative among Palestinians and throughout the region. The invasion and occupation of Iraq in 2003 has only fomented more Islamism.

- In the absence of fully developed and articulated movements, institutions, and discourses of liberalism or socialism, Islam became the discursive universe, and Islamist movements spread the message that "Islam is the solution." For some Muslims, the new Islamic ideology reduces anxiety because it is able to offer a new form of assurance, and the movement provides new forms of collective solidarity and support.

- In the context of economic, political, and ideological crisis—including unpopular state regimes and marginalized left movements—the vacuum has come to be filled by Islamist leaders and discourses, whether fundamentalist, pietistic, or extremist.

- In the new ideological formation, tradition is both exalted and frequently invented. Although there are traditional forms of modest dress throughout the Muslim world, often reflecting local cultures and histories, Islamists in the 1980s began to promote a uniform kind of veiling, consisting largely of all-encompassing dark clothing. A recurrent theme was that Islamic identity is in danger; Muslims had to return to a fixed tradition; identity was incumbent upon women's behavior, dress, appearance; and Muslim personal laws were necessary at the level of the state (in the case of majority-Muslim societies) or in the community (in the case of minority-Muslim groups).

- Islamist movements are a product of the contradictions of transition and modernization; they also result from the North–South contention and hegemonic intrusions in the Muslim world; and they are political projects concerned with power in what they view as a repressive, unjust, and un-Islamic order. Culture, religion, and identity act both as defense mechanisms and as means by which the new order is to be shaped.

GLOBALIZING ISLAMISM

We may refer to a global Islamist movement even though many movements are locally or nationally based. The term "global" describes the scale, scope, and reach of Islamism, and acknowledges that many Islamists engage in cross-border communication, coordination, solidarity, and direct action. Some scholars distinguish between local and transnational Islamism, demarcating al-Qaeda from, for example, Hamas or Hezbollah. Both forms, however, have roots in theology, history, and contemporary events.

Fawaz Gerges and others have documented the rise of transnational Islamism, noting the importance of the jihad in Afghanistan in the 1980s, supported at the time by the United States. Steeped in Sayyid Qutb's revisions of the classical doctrine of jihad, Islamists aimed to target "apostate" Muslim rulers who were not enforcing sharia; these were the "near enemy." In the 1980s and early 1990s, the national jihad in Afghanistan took a global turn when thousands of young Muslims poured into Afghanistan to join it; they were allowed to do so by governments that either wished to rid themselves of unruly young men or genuinely desired the downfall of a left-wing state in a Muslim-majority country. When the "Afghan Arabs" returned home (for example, to Algeria, Egypt, Jordan), they triggered bloody confrontations with the state. Al-Qaeda was formed in the years following Iraqi ruler Saddam Hussein's invasion of Kuwait in 1990 and the subsequent events. Osama bin Laden, a Saudi citizen from a rich family, was angry that the Saudi government had selected the U.S. Army rather than his own militia to rout Saddam Hussein in Kuwait, and he was especially provoked by the presence of U.S. troops on Saudi soil. Expelled in 1991, he went to Sudan until 1996, then to Afghanistan to be harbored by the Taliban, who by that time had replaced the U.S.-supported mujahideen. In Afghanistan, Bin Laden and Ayman al-Zawahiri, his Egyptian-born deputy, shifted attention to the "far enemy": the United States. In 1998 they publicly declared the creation of a transnational network called the International Front for Jihad against Jews and Crusaders.[16] The attacks on the United States on September 11, 2001, were carried out by nineteen young men, fifteen of whom were from Saudi Arabia.[17] The repercussions of the U.S. and Saudi support for the Afghan jihad in the 1980s have been termed "blowback."

In distinguishing between transnational and local Islamists, Gerges points out that many national Islamists were angered by 9/11 because it compromised their position in Europe, where they had sought refuge from government repression in the 1990s. Gerges surveys a wide range of literature published by Islamists and national jihadists that is bitterly critical of the transnational jihad. Nonetheless, local and transnational Islamists tend to articulate similar grievances.

All Islamists have been inspired by Sayyid Qutb's writings, but transnational jihadists take special inspiration from his book *Jahiliyyat al-Qarn al-Ishrin* (The jahiliyya of the twentieth century), which implies that now that Western modernity has come full circle to the *jahili* condition, the Arabs and the Muslims should lead humanity once more out of the *jahiliyya* created by Europe and defended by the West in general. Islamists tend to blame the spread of Western values and practices for a wide variety of social and economic ills, including rising unemployment, stagnant economic development, soaring debt, housing shortages, and dwindling public social and welfare expenditures. Western values are also blamed for what Islamists see as the breakdown of the traditional Muslim family.[18] Blaming Western influence for such developments is, as Wiktorowicz notes, "an important component of most Islamic movement diagnostic frames."[19] It follows that the solution is the return to or strengthening of Islamic values, norms, and laws.

For the moderate Islamist, the answer is peaceful "regime change" within the Muslim world through parliamentary means and the gradual Islamization of key social institutions. This includes a call for adherence to Muslim family laws and the sharia as the guide to personal and public behavior. For the radical Islamist, it is a short step from the view of "Islam in danger from the West" to the taking up of arms against Western targets and their domestic allies. Such is the motivation behind, inter alia, the Islamist revolution against the Shah in Iran (and later against the left in Iran), the assassination of Egyptian president Anwar Sadat, the targeting of secular intellectuals in Egypt and Turkey, the violent revolt in Algeria in the 1990s, and the Red Mosque affair in Pakistan in 2007. The view of Islam in danger also is behind the rise of transnational networks of militant Islamists, including but not limited to al-Qaeda. In these cases, violence becomes the form of contention.

Islamism also has been globalized through migration. The migration of large populations of Muslims to the West, largely for economic reasons, has created both an existential burden and an opportunity structure. One aspect of the burden is to try to live a meaningful life in countries that are secularized and have values and practices that are deemed inimical to Muslim values. This leads to difficulties in integration and to antipathy from the native population. In Europe, therefore, there has been much discussion of what is often framed as the problem of Muslim integration, and sometimes as "Islamophobia." The opportunity structure of Western tolerance and pluralism has meant that Muslim immigrants have been able to practice their faith openly, in highly visible ways such as building mosques and faith-based schools; wearing veils; spilling out onto the streets during prayers; establishing halal meat stores; building Islamic charities and other associations; and proselytizing and seeking converts for the Islamic faith. This has not always been well received by natives, but it has created or reinforced a collective identity among a certain section of the immigrant population as "Muslims" or even as "fighters for Islam."[20]

How have states, or other elements of the opportunity structure, contributed to the making of a globalized Islam? And what is the relationship between states and violent contention? In some cases, Muslim elites become involved or encourage Islamist contention to enhance their own credentials, undermine the organized left, or distract the public from pressing socio-economic issues. We have seen that this was a strategy deployed by states and political elites in many Middle Eastern countries in the 1970s and 1980s. The fatwa, or religious edict, issued against Indian-British writer Salman Rushdie in early 1989 by Ayatollah Khomeini, leader of Iran's Islamic revolution, helped to globalize Islam by mobilizing militants across the world to protest what Khomeini claimed to be an affront to the Quran and the Prophet. The mass media and elite complicity helped to galvanize violent contention. In his study of the 2006 Danish cartoons conflict, Thomas Olesen shows how elites and the mass media were the prime movers in the transnational escalation of the controversy. Street manifestations such as riots and demonstrations took place first in Palestine and Kuwait, and then in Yemen, Indonesia, Turkey, Syria, Lebanon, Afghanistan, Iran, Egypt, and the Philippines. Danish embassies in Damascus and Beirut were set on fire. Egyptian state-owned newspapers called for a boycott of Danish goods, calling the cartoons "a crime against the Muslim world."[21] This exemplifies the role played by strong media and political opportunity structures in transnational collective action. It reveals, too, the periodic complicity between regimes and Islamist movements.

The literature on social movements suggests that state repression could have a pre-emptive or dampening effect on collective action. Conversely, state repression could force contenders to turn to violent methods. John Entelis, a scholar of North African politics, views Algeria's Front Islamique du Salut (FIS) as a "quintessential . . . Islamist reformist movement" and sees the Algerian regime as conforming to a widespread practice of confrontation that "unleashed a much more virulent form of Islamic radicalism."[22] In their joint work and separate writings on Islamic activism and on Muslim rebellions, Wiktorowicz and Hafez argue that the use of violence by groups as varied as the Armed Islamic Group (GIA) in Algeria, the Gama'a Islamiyya (Islamic Group) in Egypt, the Palestinian Hamas, and Shiites who revolted during the 1990s in Bahrain "was, to a large extent, a tactical response to shifting opportunity structures and emerged under particular conditions and circumstances."[23] Hafez shows how the GIA moved toward "a growing belief in total war" when the Islamist movement was excluded from institutional politics and suffered indiscriminate state repression.[24] Here he is referring to the events of 1992, in which the ruling party, supported by the military, annulled the results of elections that favored the Front Islamique du Salut and subsequently banned the FIS. A similar argument has been made for Egypt's Gama'a Islamiyya. Hafez and Wiktorowicz maintain that "the cycle of violence in Egypt began largely in response to a broad crackdown on the Islamic movement that targeted moderates, radicals, and a number of tangential bystanders. The crackdown included arrests, hostage taking, torture, executions, and other forms of state violence."[25] There and elsewhere, it is argued, Islamist insurgencies are provoked by state-sponsored exclusion, marginalization, and repression.

But there is more to the cycle of Islamist contentious politics than state repression, and a rather complex and almost symbiotic relationship exists between states and Islamist movements. Efforts by political elites to incorporate or co-opt Islamist institutions between the 1950s and 1970s were only partially or temporarily successful, for radical elements that saw the society or state as insufficiently Islamic would periodically assert themselves. Islamists in Algeria, after all, had been encouraged by their experience in Afghanistan, and were allowed to operate openly in the 1980s. Algerian feminists were alarmed when Islamists began to bully unveiled women in the districts where they predominated. Feminists began to mobilize when the new government of Chadli Bendjedid acquiesced to Islamist pressure and pushed through a very conservative family law.[26] Even Hafez admits that the Algerian GIA—whose revolt against the state in the 1990s featured wanton and breathtaking brutality against civilians and foreigners—did not resort to violence due to the cancellation of the election results and the banning of the FIS. "On the contrary, it viewed its 'jihad' as a broader struggle to rid the Muslim world of un-Islamic rulers and establish the 'rule of God.'"[27] In the GIA's own words, expressed in a 1993 communiqué: "Our struggle is with infidelism and its supporters beginning with France and ending with the leader of international terrorism, 'the United States of Terrorism,' its ally Israel, and among them the apostate ruling regime in our land."[28] Four years later, the group expressed the following views in a London-based Islamist paper:

> The infidelism and apostasy of this hypocrite nation that turned away from backing and supporting the mujahideen will not bend our determination and will not hurt us at all, God willing. . . All the killing and slaughter, the massacres, the displacement [of people], the burnings, the kidnappings . . . are an offering to God.[29]

While state repression clearly played a role in exacerbating societal strains and political grievances, the GIA's extreme violence, including violence against women, suggests a kind of pathology and misogyny rather far removed from rational, cost-benefit calculations.

Similarly, Egyptian Islamists not only targeted symbols of the state, such as financial centers and the tourism industry; they also killed tourists, Egyptian Christians (Copts), and secular intellectuals. Sociologist Jeff Goodwin makes an elegant argument that identifies "categorical terrorism," or forms of extreme violence that deliberately target civilians, as a strategy taken up in a context of "indiscriminate state repression" and "civilian complicity." Terrorism thus becomes a way of punishing mass passivity or complicity with the state. Goodwin applies this framework to the actions of militants in French Algeria, the West Bank and Gaza, and Chechnya. Also, to a certain extent, he employs this conceptual lens in looking at al-Qaeda's attacks of September 11. While persuasive on one level, Goodwin's theory basically posits that militants—like repressive states or occupying powers—can and do engage in collective punishment to achieve their goals and assert their authority.[30]

It is true that many liberation movements and social revolutions have entailed armed struggles as a key tactic. Research on revolutions shows that the more accessible the state, the less likely it is to unify opposition behind a violent strategy.[31] And yet the flagrant language and actions of the GIA and similar groups help both analysts and progressives to clarify the distinction between the legitimate actions of a liberation movement and the illegitimate actions of terrorists.

At the same time, the brazen actions and self-confident language of the GIA suggest that the struggle in Algeria should be viewed in the larger context of the growth of transnational Islamism. After all, the 1990s were the decade of transition on a world scale, defined by the end of the Soviet Union and the collapse of communist ideology; the assumption of power in 1992 by the Afghan mujahideen (who had been supported by the United States for over a decade); the attacks on U.S. marines in Lebanon and the withdrawal of American troops; the breakup of formerly socialist Yugoslavia; the Islamist revolt in Chechnya; spectacular terrorist assaults in various parts of the world, including Tanzania and Kenya; and the emergence of the Taliban in Afghanistan following their 1996 overthrow of the mujahideen. The Taliban, it will be recalled, harbored Osama bin Laden following his expulsion from Sudan.

Transnational Islam was made possible by the post–Cold War world order, along with the opportunities afforded by globalization's accoutrements, notably rapid communications via the Internet. Geographic reordering and collapsed states allowed for the distribution of arms and militants across porous borders. Meanwhile, Muslim grievances were disseminated across the Muslim world via the Internet and Arabic-language media. The grievances included the dire effects of the UN sanctions against Iraq following Saddam Hussein's invasion of Kuwait; the presence of U.S. troops in Muslim lands (Kuwait, Saudi Arabia, Lebanon); the continuing injustices suffered by Palestinians at the hands of Israel; the killing of Chechens, Bosnians, and Kosovars; and the United States' bombing of what turned out to be a pharmaceutical factory in Khartoum, conducted during the search for Osama bin Laden. In the new millennium, nineteen young Arab men plotted to attack symbols of American power in the United States. This was GIA on a transnational, global scale.

Mobilizing structures thus developed from nationally based to transnational and often coordinated. If the language, goals, and methods of Algeria's GIA have strong parallels with those of al-Qaeda, it is likely that some GIA activists went on to join al-Qaeda's transnational network in the new millennium. Islamists from Egypt, Jordan, Morocco, Tunisia, Pakistan, and elsewhere also joined the al-Qaeda network, while radicalized youth among second-generation Muslim immigrants in Europe undertook terrorist acts in Europe. Violence became the tactic of choice of transnational jihadist Islamism, as evidenced by the bombings of commuters in London and in Madrid, as well as by the bombings in Bali, Casablanca, Algiers, and Baghdad.

MODERATE AND PARLIAMENTARY ISLAMIST
MOVEMENTS: WHAT OF THE GRAY ZONES?

The preceding narrative pertains to the emergence, resources, frames, collective action repertoires, and other defining features of militant Islamist networks. What of moderate or parliamentary Islamism? Scholars and political analysts have sought to distinguish moderate from militant Islamist groups. Frame alignment among moderate Islamists is distinctive and diverges from that of militant Islamists, as they address different audiences, both domestic and international. In general, moderate Islamists eschew violence as a tactic to gain political or state power; they take part in electoral politics and field candidates, sometimes openly and other times through independents; and they take an active part in civil society associations. In Turkey, for example, moderate Islamists claim to accept the secular and republican ideals of modern Turkey's founder Kemal Ataturk. In Egypt, the Muslim Brotherhood has claimed to favor democracy and civil rights for all citizens. In Europe, moderates draw on human rights and anti-discrimination frames to claim the right to veil and build mosques. Some scholars have therefore pondered the possibility that moderate, reformist Islam evinces similarities either to Christian liberation theology or to the Christian-democratic (conservative) political parties of Europe.

Does Turkey's ruling Islamist party fall within the radical or the liberal category? And is there any connection between liberal Islamists and the Christian groups that have espoused "liberation theology," with its pro-poor activism and anti-capitalist critique? Writing about the now-defunct Refah [Welfare] Party that made electoral headway in the 1990s before it was banned by the Turkish military, Turkish sociologist Haldun Gulalp points out:

> While liberation theology constitutes a novel interpretation of Christianity from a socialist perspective, Welfare's Islamism focused on the question of cultural superiority or inferiority. . . . Turkey's political Islam . . . was concerned with a cultural project and attempted to mobilize people by addressing their class interests in order to effect that project. . . . Welfare used class-related issues as a vehicle to promote a project of change in lifestyle and to establish its own version of an "Islam" society.[32]

Gulalp goes on to argue that moderate Islamist movements are part of the phenomenon of post-modernist "new social movements" in that they are focused on issues of culture, identity, and lifestyle rather than class and ideology.

In discussing the social bases of Turkey's Islamism, Gulalp links mobilization and recruitment to broad structural changes. He notes, correctly, that the rise of Islamism coincided with the decline of the Keynesian economic project, Fordist industrialization, and the welfare state, with its attendant focus on the working class. Islamism gained prominence concurrently with the economic trends of privatization, subcontracting, and entrepreneurship, which favor property owners and small businesspeople. In Turkey, while political power remained in the hands of bureaucratic, military, and political elites, economic power was shifting to the increasingly growing private sector. The Islamist movement claimed to be the voice of the owners of small and medium-sized businesses, who complained of inadequate financial support by the state. Gradually this movement nudged its way from the fringes to the centers of political power. Thus, in contrast to Latin American–style liberation theology, with its focus on the poor and its demand for redistribution, Turkey's Islamists created a new capitalist culture. Their vision esteemed both business and Islamic lifestyle norms such as the wearing of the veil, the prohibition of alcohol, and attention to religious schooling. Gulalp notes that the Islamist party's discourse of "justice" appealed to working-class voters, even though the party was in reality an extension of the neoliberal project.[33]

Written from a left-wing perspective, Gulalp's analysis elucidates the compatibility of Islamism with neoliberalism—even if Islamists may oppose other aspects of globalization. Likewise, other analysts have drawn attention to ambivalences, ambiguities, or inconsistencies in the discourses and practices of moderate Islamists. Brown, Hamzawy, and Ottaway refer to these ambiguities as the "gray zones," which they attribute to

> the character of these movements as political and religious organizations, the rise of a new generation of activists, and the contradictions of the broader sociopolitical context of the countries where they operate. As a result, there is no guarantee that time will automatically lead to the elimination of the gray zones and that non-violent Islamic organizations will continue to evolve in a liberal direction. Rather, the outcome is still uncertain, and it will be determined by how the political situation evolves.[34]

What of Egypt's Muslim Brotherhood (Ikhwan), considered the world's largest, oldest, and most influential Islamist organization? Founded by Hassan al-Banna, the Brotherhood was for decades a radical movement bent on overthrowing the secular Egyptian regime and replacing it with an Islamic state. As noted, an early leading figure, Sayyid Qutb, became even more radicalized after a trip to the United States and upon his return wrote fiery pamphlets and books. For his role in fomenting violent resistance, he was executed by the government of Gamal Abdel Nasser; the Brotherhood has been banned since 1954. Sympathizers portray Egypt's Muslim groups as pressure groups oriented toward specific political interests and operating within and upon a regime whose mix of repression, acculturation, and semi-toleration has effectively limited their room for maneuver.[35] Others point out that the Brotherhood maintains its societal and political presence through a sympathetic judiciary, al-Azhar University and theological seminary, adherents in professional syndicates, and parliamentary candidates running as independents. As well as having influential branches around the world, the Brotherhood is Egypt's strongest opposition to President Hosni Mubarak, who has ruled as an autocrat since 1981 and is a key U.S. ally. Estimates of the Brotherhood's Egyptian membership range from one hundred thousand to four hundred thousand.[36]

The metamorphosis of the Egyptian Muslim Brothers from a religious mass movement to a seemingly modern political party has its roots in the changing political economy of the 1980s, with the deterioration of public services, declining real wages, and rising unemployment. Although the Brotherhood distanced itself from some of the more rigid doctrines of its founder, it continued to proffer its slogan "Islam Is the Solution" and to call for adherence to the sharia. Shrewd political maneuvers, including extensive participation in local councils, grassroots associations, and syndicates, assured electoral gains by moderate Islamists associated with the Muslim Brothers. The Brotherhood shocked the ruling National Democratic Party and Western observers in 2005 by winning one-fifth of the seats in the Egyptian Parliament through independent proxies. The Muslim Brothers' association with al-Azhar, a site of fundamentalist Islam as well as a university, assures the movement of both legitimacy and an important mobilizing structure.

In recent years the Brotherhood has issued statements in support of democracy and the rights of women and religious minorities. But the gray zones persist, with analysts identifying ambiguities and inconsistencies in their positions on the application of Islamic law; the use of violence; political pluralism; civil and political rights; equality and rights of women; and equality and rights of religious minorities.[37] In 2007 the Supreme Guide of Egypt's Muslim Brotherhood, Mohamed Mahdi Akef, was responsible for the draft of the Brotherhood's first political platform. Among other things, it advocated banning women and Coptic Christians, who make up one-tenth of Egypt's population, from becoming president, and it raised the specter of an Iran-style religious council. Akef and his associates viewed globalization as naked U.S. ambition, and regarded Western democracy as "subservient to whims of the masses, without moral absolutes."[38] Apart from vague references to social justice, the Muslim Brotherhood is not particularly interested in economic issues and has not developed a critique of Egypt's neoliberal economic strategy. According to El-Ghobashy, "They still grant culture and identity issues pride of place in their platform."[39]

Writing about political Islam in general, Graham Fuller identifies three obstacles to its liberal evolution. The first comes from the local political scene, where Islamists are routinely suppressed, jailed, tortured, and executed. Such circumstances encourage the emergence of secret, conspiratorial, and often armed groups rather than liberal ones. The second obstacle, he writes, comes from international politics, which often pushes Islamist parties and movements, including Muslim national liberation movements, in a militant direction. The third "comes from the Islamists' own long list of grievances against the forces and policies perceived to be holding Muslims back in the contemporary world, many of them associated with liberalism's supposed avatar, the United States."[40]

Scholars of Middle East politics continue to debate the prospects of a liberal, reformist, and democratic Islamist movement, and its place within the political process. Jillian Schwedler examines shifting discourses and practices of Islamist parties in Jordan and Yemen as evidence of real moderation. Vickie Langohr points out that what is on offer to Islamist movements in most countries is participation in electoral contests for political office in state systems that remain highly authoritarian.[41] Still, with a collective action repertoire of marches, rallies, banners, and petitions, Islamist parties have made headway in a number of Muslim-majority countries, including Egypt, Turkey, Morocco, Jordan, Palestine, Yemen, Indonesia, and Malaysia.

MOBILIZING STRUCTURES
AND CULTURAL FRAMES

Social movement theorizing has identified the importance of informal ties and social networks to recruitment and movement formation and has focused much attention on the role and formation of organizations, networks, informal groups, and other mobilizing structures. With respect to Islamist movements, some of the principal vehicles by which adherents are recruited and supporters attracted are mosques, *madrassas* (religious schools), *nadwas* (Quranic study groups), and charities. In some cases and countries, the bazaar or *souk* also has played a role, mainly through its partnership with the mosque. In turn, these institutions constitute an "organizational infrastructure" for Islamist movements both local and transnational.

In much the same way that churches have played a role in mobilizing people and framing protest in the United States, Eastern Europe, South Africa, and elsewhere, mosques have been both places of worship and sites of religio-political mobilizations. The mosque was a key institution for the mobilization of protest in the years that led to the 1979 Iranian revolution, and also was used by the Islamist state for the distribution of ration coupons during the war with Iraq in the 1980s. Across the Muslim world, the mosque and its attendant institutions such as the madrassa, the nadwa, and charitable foundations connect communities of believers but also provide a base from which to organize and mobilize.[42] Judith Harik describes how Lebanon's Hezbollah, which is both a political party and a militant Islamist organization, built a network of charities and how that investment in welfare organizations translated into electoral gains at the grassroots level, especially in the southern suburb of Beirut. Janine Clark's study of Islamist charities and social welfare organizations in Egypt, Jordan, and Yemen demonstrates their success with poor and middle-class citizens alike. Providing assistance with marriage, health care, and schooling, these and other "Islamic social institutions" have proved critical in offering marginalized and disaffected citizens both symbolic and material rewards, thus ensuring steady recruitment to the Islamist cause.[43] Charities and nadwas are especially successful at mobilizing women and providing them with roles to play within the Islamist movement or party, such as fundraising for the poor during Ramadan and carrying out *da'wa*, or preaching. In some countries (Egypt is a notable example), Islamist influence has extended to professional and student associations that are able to build transnational ties of solidarity with confrères. Elsewhere (for example, Jordan, Turkey, Malaysia, Indonesia, Palestine, Yemen) Islamists have mobilized support, disseminated their messages, and influenced public policy through political parties as well as the more traditional institutions. As Wiktorowicz correctly notes, Islamic movements have emerged as a dominant opposition in the Muslim world because they command more societal institutions and resources than other movements, and because of their ability to tap religious resources.[44]

The more radical and jihadist Islamists similarly recruit members and supporters and raise funds through mosques, madrassas, religious study groups, and charities, as well as through social and family ties. In Europe, radical mosques and imams with fiery messages appealed to disaffected young men, who went on to join cells or engaged in militant activism to defend what they felt were slurs or attacks on Islam. In England, they formed groups such as Tablighi Jamaat and al-Muhajiroun.[45] Increasingly porous borders in Europe facilitated interactions between contacts, some of whom were able to engage in bombings and other violent acts. Failed or fragile states elsewhere—such as in Afghanistan, Iraq, and Sudan—enable Islamist militants to travel for purposes of recruitment, training, or militant action.

The Internet is another mobilizing vehicle, as well as a framing tool. Islamists have made effective use of the new computer technologies for purposes of information exchange, dissemination of their message, and projection of desired symbols and images. Numerous websites are controlled by local as well as transnational Islamists, enabling a kind of virtual activism. Indeed, al-Qaeda has a media wing, called al-Sahib. In December 2007, Ayman al-Zawahiri, Osama bin Laden's deputy, invited subscribers to jihadist websites to post questions for al-Qaeda's leadership, and promised that answers would be provided by mid-January 2008. In the same message inviting postings, Zawahiri emphasized the importance of "jihadi information media," saying they were "waging an extremely critical battle against the Crusader-Zionist enemy." He noted that information "used to be the exclusive domain of . . . the official government media and the . . . media which claim to be free and non-governmental."[46] In early January 2008, an Islamist website posted a video featuring al-Qaeda's American-born member Adam Gadahn, who urged fighters to meet President Bush with bombs when he visited the Middle East later that month.[47] The many Islamist websites function as sites of self-advertisement, recruitment, and communication. In this they are sometimes helped by some Arab media. In broadcasting Islamist messages and images, al-Jazeera and al-Arabiyya, for example, help disseminate the idea that Islam and Muslims are in danger and need to fight back. As Manfred Steger has noted, Arab satellite media are part of a "chain of global interdependencies and interconnections" that make possible the instant broadcast of messages and images, including those of militant Islamists. What is more, "Bin Laden may have denounced the forces of modernity with great conviction, but the smooth operation of his entire organization was entirely dependent on advanced forms of technology developed in the last two decades of the twentieth century."[48]

Thus over and above the effective use of mobilizing structures, Islamists have taken advantage of the opportunities afforded by globalization—specifically, the Internet, global media, and shifting geographies—to organize, build networks, coordinate activities, disseminate their message, and otherwise engage in collective action. Indeed, the making of an Islamist transnational public sphere has been facilitated by globalization. And this discursive space has been taken up by themes such as attacks on Islam, the occupations of Iraq, Afghanistan, and Palestine, corrupt and dictatorial regimes, and the need to proselytize Islam and spread the faith across the globe.

For millions of Muslims worldwide, Islam is practiced in peace and with quiet dignity. Those who turn to violent contention, however, can justify their actions by selective recourse to Islamic scriptures regarding the imperative to defend Islam against its enemies. As sociologist Farhad Khosrokhavar has explained, Islamic martyrdom differs from Christian martyrdom in that it is an offensive response (rather than a passive one) to ward off challenges to the religion and thereby protect what is cherished and valued.[49] Concerns about cultural invasion, or the Israeli occupation of Palestinian land, or the presence of "infidel" soldiers and "crusaders" in Saudi Arabia, Afghanistan, and Iraq, or even relatively minor events such as satirical cartoons about the Prophet Muhammad in a Danish newspaper or the awarding of a British medal of honor to the writer Salman Rushdie—these can trigger intense emotions and strong beliefs about insults to Islam, a war against Islam, and the religiously mandated imperative to defend the faith militarily. In this way, Muslim militants can draw on a ready-made cultural frame while also utilizing the existing organizational infrastructure.

REPERTOIRES OF CONTENTION: ISLAMIST AND LEFT-WING TERRORISTS

Can we better understand contemporary militant Islamism by way of comparison with other militant groups? Could Islamist terrorism represent not a growing worldwide movement but a futile attempt at power? The Syrian political philosopher Sadik Al-Azm has compared Islamist terror networks to those of the extreme left in Europe in the 1970s.[50] The latter's acts included the abduction and murder of the German industrialist Hans Martin Schleyer by the Baader-Meinhof gang in the summer of 1977 and the similar abduction and assassination, a year later, of Aldo Moro, the dean of

Italy's senior political leaders after World War II, by the Italian Red Brigades. The left-wing terrorism of the 1970s in Europe, Al-Azm maintains, was a "desperate attempt to break out of the historical impasse and terminal structural crisis reached by communism, radical labor movements, Third Worldism, and revolutionary trends everywhere, by resorting to violent *action directe* of the most extraordinary and phenomenal kind." The terrorism of that period, he argues, was "a) the then barely viable manifestation of that impasse and crisis, and b) the prelude to the final demise of all those movements and trends including world communism itself."[51]

Similarly, "the *action directes* Islamists have also given up on contemporary Muslim society, its socio-political movements, the spontaneous religiosity of the masses, their endemic false consciousness, mainstream Islamic organizations, the attention of the original and traditional Society of Muslim Brothers (from which they generally hail in the same way the original *action directes* hailed from European communism)." They have rejected all this, he writes, in favor of "their own brand of blind and spectacular activism, also heedless and contemptuous of consequences, long-term calculations of the chances of success or failure and so on." This kind of politics takes the form of "local attacks, intermittent skirmishes, guerrilla raids, random insurrections, senseless resistances, impatient outbursts, anarchistic assaults, and sudden uprisings." Al-Azm refers to "an Islamist impatient rejection of and contempt for politics in almost any form: conventional, radical, agitational and/or revolutionary in favor of the violent tactics of nihilism and despair. For them, the only other alternatives available are either cooptation or plain withdrawal or an admission of defeat." The *action directe* Islamists, like their European counterparts, "evince a sense of entrapment within an alien and alienating monolithic socio-political reality."[52] Al-Azm continues:

> With maximalist Islamism we get *action directe* terrorism on a global scale where the only kind of politics permitted is direct and immediate armed attack against the enemy. The assumption in all this is that such apocalyptic Islamist self-assertion will a) explode the obstacles blocking the way to the global triumph of Islam, b) overcome the structural impasse in which the Islamist project finds itself at present, c) develop better objective conditions for the success of that project, d) catalyze the Muslim people's energies in its favor, and e) create poles of attraction around which the Muslims of the world could immediately rally, for example the Al-Qaeda set of networks, organizations, training camps, etc., and the Taliban model of the supposedly first authentic Muslim society and government in modern times.[53]

While the analogy is useful in showing how repertoires of violent contention can travel from one geo-cultural space to another, the scale of European extremist left-wing violence was far smaller, and its time span shorter, than that of contemporary Islamism. This may be because the European extremists were more isolated, less networked, and less popular than contemporary Islamists; and they had fewer resources, including culturally resonant frames, at their disposal.

CONCLUSION

Political Islam appeared on the international stage in the late 1970s in the context of specific national and global opportunities and includes an array of locally based groups and transnationally active networks. Some groups attempt the overthrow of local regimes; others are long entrenched in cooperative relations with them; yet others seek social, political, and legal reforms. Moderate Islamists take part in the electoral process and promote democracy to widen their social base and advance their interests; radicals rail against national and international injustices and call for strict adherence to Islam; extremists spread their message and assert themselves through violence, often spectacular. Many jihadists around the world enjoy sufficient "street credibility" to sway younger hearts and minds. Many won their spurs as fighters in the American-backed campaign against the Soviet intervention in Afghanistan.

Since the late 1970s, Islamists of different orientations have come to power in Iran, Pakistan, Bangladesh, Sudan, Afghanistan, and Turkey; and in parts of Nigeria, Malaysia, and Indonesia. As Middle Eastern and other states in the Muslim world have expanded, members of Islamist movements, in their capacity as well-educated members of their societies, have become employees of state bureaucracies. In Turkey, the Islamist movement had placed a sizable number of its members in the state bureaucracy by the mid-1990s. In Jordan, Islamic Action Front members were awarded the Ministry of Education. These developments have given rise to questions about the compatibility of Islamism with democracy and human rights. To date, no Islamist movement has been instrumental in the transition from authoritarianism to democracy and civil liberties. As two scholars associated with liberal Islam note: "The challenge for Muslims is how to capture the massive dissonances of these times by retrieving the depth of faith without slipping into monasticism or zealotry. A democratizing and synthesizing Islam, reflecting influences from the bottom, is better placed to respond to globalization."[54] As we have seen, even moderate and parliamentary Islamists evince ambiguities and ambivalences in their views and practices on minority rights, women's rights, and various social freedoms. In this respect, Islamist movements would seem to be at the opposite end of the spectrum from feminist and global justice movements.

The Islamist focus on the West as the source of all ills—economic, political, and cultural—is of course the mirror image of the Huntington thesis of "the clash of civilizations" whereby the most profound clash is that between Islam and the West.[55] In both cases, cultural values and norms are emphasized as pre-eminent, and seen to be at stake. In the Huntington perspective, the world of Islam is at odds with Western notions of democracy, tolerance, and pluralism. The solution is to keep a distance, close ranks, and protect Western values. In the Islamist perspective, the West is responsible—through such ills as secularism, feminism, gay liberation, and support for repressive regimes—for undermining Muslim societies and exerting control over them. The solution is to reject Western values and institutions and adhere strictly to Islamic laws, norms, and institutions. Both arguments essentialize religion and culture, and cast the religio-cultural differences between Islam and the West in sharp relief.

Globalization processes have provided both grievances and opportunities for the emergence and growth of Islamist movements. Concerns over cultural invasion, political and military interventions in Muslim lands, and economic difficulties have galvanized militant Muslims, while the Internet has allowed them to disseminate their messages, coordinate activities, recruit followers, and maintain networks. If Islam is a world religion, Islamism has become a globalized ideology and movement.

CHAPTER 4

FEMINISM ON A WORLD SCALE

The women's rights movement has been the subject of considerable scholarly analysis. Feminist theorizing has focused on national-level factors such as the growth of the population of educated women with grievances about their second-class citizenship; varieties of feminism; the evolution of women's movements and campaigns; and cross-regional similarities and differences in mobilizing structures and strategies.[1]

Since the 1990s a growing literature has connected women's movements and organizations to global processes such as the role of international organizations or the United Nations Decade on Women, and it has examined the ways that women's organizations engage with the world of public policy. While not all feminists agree on the matter, many argue that "the women's movement" is a global phenomenon, and that despite cultural differences, country specificities, and organizational priorities, there are observed similarities in the ways that women's rights activists frame their grievances and demands, form networks and organizations, and engage with state and intergovernmental institutions.[2] Some of these similarities include adoption of discourses of women's human rights and gender equality; references to international agreements such as the Convention on the Elimination of All Forms of Discrimination Against Women (CEDAW) and the Beijing Platform for Action; campaigns for legal and policy reforms to ensure women's civil, political, and social rights; solidarity and networking across borders; and coalitions with other civil society groups. Another observation is that women's rights activists—whether in South Asia, Latin America, the Middle East, or North Africa—are opposed to "fundamentalist" discourses and agendas and espouse feminist discourses and goals, whether explicitly or implicitly. Valerie Sperling, Myra Marx Ferree, and Barbara Risman have correctly concluded that "feminist action" is an appropriate term to define "that in which the participants explicitly place value on challenging gender hierarchy and changing women's social status, whether they adopt or reject the feminist label."[3] Similarly, Mary Hawkesworth defines "global feminist activism" as international feminist mobilizations involving women in more than one country or region "who seek to forge a collective identity among women and to improve the condition of women."[4] Moghadam has identified such mobilizations as "transnational feminist networks" that advocate for women's participation and rights while also engaging critically with policy and legal issues and with states, international organizations, and institutions of global governance.[5]

Like the Islamist movement studied in the previous chapter and the global justice movement to be examined in the next, the women's movement is transnational and diverse, exhibiting the segmentary, polycentric, and reticulate features that Gerlach identified as common to many social movements (see chapter 1). These features of the global women's movement were especially evident during the Fourth World Conference on Women, which took place in Beijing, China, in September 1995. For three weeks, women's groups from across the world met in China to take part in the massive non-governmental forum that preceded but also overlapped with the official, intergovernmental conference. At the latter, those women's groups with UN accreditation were able to enter conference halls, lobby delegates, disseminate their literature, and hold rallies. This was hardly a movement with a center or a bureaucracy or a hierarchy. It was a movement of movements, albeit highly networked. And although the women's groups at Beijing had something to say about an array of issues,[6] they also had common grievances concerning war, peace, fundamentalisms, and the new economic order.

This chapter examines the relationship between globalization and the global women's movement, with a focus on three types of transnational feminist networks (TFNs) that emerged in the 1980s and continue to be active to this day. Discussed in this chapter are networks that target the neoliberal economic policy agenda; those that focus on fundamentalism and insist on women's human rights, especially in the Muslim world; and women's peace groups that target conflict, war, and empire. We begin with a discussion of the global context and the opportunity structure(s) within which transnational feminism emerged.

THE ROAD TO TRANSNATIONAL FEMINISM

Chapter 1 described the precursors to the contemporary women's movement, including international women's organizations and campaigns of the early twentieth century. In mid-century the women's movement began to diverge, grouping itself within national boundaries or economic zones, emphasizing different priorities, and aligning with divergent ideological currents. In particular, North–South differences became pronounced as feminists in the core countries and those in the developing world expressed radically different grievances and formed divergent strategies.

The women's movement of the second wave, which began in North America and Europe in the 1960s, consisted of feminist groups that emerged within national borders and addressed themselves to their own nation-states, governments, employers, male colleagues, and kin. As women's groups expanded across the globe, they remained primarily nationally based and nationally oriented. Feminist groups encompassed liberal, radical, Marxist, and socialist ideologies, and these political differences constituted one form of division within feminism. The Cold War cast a shadow on feminist solidarity, in the form of the East–West divide; there was, for the most part, antipathy between women's groups aligned with the communist movement and liberal feminist groups aligned with the so-called Free World. Another division took the form of North–South, or First World–Third World, differences in terms of prioritizing feminist issues; many First World feminists saw legal equality and reproductive rights as key feminist demands and goals, while many Third World feminists emphasized underdevelopment, colonialism, and imperialism as obstacles to women's advancement. Disagreements over what constituted top-priority feminist issues came to the fore at the beginning of the United Nations' Decade for Women, and especially at its first and second world conferences on women, which took place in Mexico City in 1975 and in Copenhagen in 1980, respectively. The disagreements at the Mexico City and Copenhagen conferences pitted women activists from the North and from the South against each other, and revolved around prioritizing issues of legal equality and personal choice versus issues pertaining to global economic and political hierarchies.[7]

A shift in the nature and orientation of international feminism began to take place in the mid-1980s, during preparations for the third UN world conference on women, which was held in Nairobi, Kenya in 1985. The shift took the form of bridge building and consensus making across regional and ideological divides, and the emergence of a women's organization of a new type. What enabled significant frame alignments to take place and new collective action repertoires to emerge in the women's movement were three critical economic and political developments within states and regions, and at the level of the world-system: the transition from Keynesian to neoliberal economics, along with a new international division of labor that relied heavily on (cheap) female labor; the decline of the welfare state in the core countries and the developmental state in the Third World; and the emergence of various forms of fundamentalist movements. These changes led to new thinking and new forms of organizing on the part of activist women in developing and developed countries alike. Let's examine these issues in more detail.

Beginning in the late 1970s, cross-national research, including studies by those working in the field of women-in-development or women-and-development (WID/WAD), showed that an ever-growing proportion of the world's women were being incorporated as cheap labor into what was variously called the capitalist world-economy, the new international division of labor, or the global assembly line.[8] Studies showed that women were gaining an increasing share of many kinds of jobs, but this was occurring in a context of growing unemployment, a decline in the social power of labor, and an increase in temporary, part-time, casual, and home-based work—that is, in the context of the shift in the capitalist world-system from Keynesian to neoliberal economic policy. Now disproportionately involved in irregular forms of employment increasingly used to maximize profits, women also remained responsible for reproductive work and domestic labor. Cutbacks in social services that were part of structural adjustment policies or the new neoliberal policy package meant that women's growing labor-market participation was not accompanied by a redistribution of domestic, household, and child care responsibilities. Rather, the changing nature of the state vis-à-vis the public sector meant the withdrawal, deterioration, or privatization of many public services used by working-class and middle-class women and their families. In addition, women remained disadvantaged in the new labor markets, in terms of wages, training, and occupational segregation. In the late 1980s, ILO economist Guy Standing termed this phenomenon the "feminization of labor." He argued that the increasing globalization of production and the pursuit of flexible forms of labor to retain or increase competitiveness, as well as changing job structures in industrial enterprises, favored the "feminization of employment" in the dual sense of an increase in the numbers of women in the labor force and a deterioration of work conditions (labor standards, income, and employment status).[9] As global restructuring expanded to encompass the former communist bloc, studies showed that women in Eastern Europe and the former Soviet Union were significantly affected by unemployment, loss of income, and privatization.[10] A body of research also emerged to address another new global phenomenon: the "feminization of poverty," or the growing female share of the population living under the poverty line.[11] Much of this research was carried out by scholar-activists with links to the women's movement, and this academic involvement had an effect on feminist strategies across the globe, including the North.

Another important development that led to the narrowing of the political and ideological divide between First World and Third World feminists was the rise of Islamic fundamentalism in Muslim countries and Hindu communalism in India. These movements sought to recuperate traditional norms and codes, including patriarchal laws and family roles for women; they put pressure on states to enforce public morality, increase religious observance, and tighten controls over women—ostensibly to protect the nation or culture from alien influences and conspiracies. In many cases there was collusion between states and the religio-political movements, usually to the detriment of women's rights.[12] Such movements alarmed feminists in the peripheral and semi-peripheral countries where the movements emerged. At the same time, feminists in the United States began to take notice of the increasing influence of the Christian right.

Divergences, therefore, began to narrow in the mid-1980s as a result of the changing environments in both the North and the South, including the rise of neoliberalism and the growth of fundamentalist movements. The new economic and political realities gradually led to a convergence of feminist perspectives across the globe: for many First World feminists, economic issues and development policy became increasingly important, and for many Third World feminists, increased attention was now directed to women's legal status, autonomy, and rights. New framings were accompanied by new mobilizing structures, notably the formation of a number of transnational feminist networks that brought together women from developed and developing countries alike to respond to economic pressures and patriarchal movements. These included Development Alternatives with Women for a New Era (DAWN), Network Women in Development Europe (WIDE), the Women's Environment and Development Organization (WEDO), Women Living Under Muslim Laws (WLUML), and the Sisterhood Is Global Institute (SIGI). Many others formed in the 1990s. They engaged in policy-oriented research, advocacy, and lobbying around issues pertaining to women and development and women's human rights. Many of the women who formed or joined the TFNs were scholar-activists who had been, and continue to be, involved in the women and development research community. With the formation of these networks and other women's activist groups, a global social movement of women was in the making. (See table 4.1.)

During this period, however, international feminism gave surprisingly little attention to one important issue: the conflict in Afghanistan and the implications for women of Western support for the Islamic–tribal alliance of the mujahideen (holy warriors). The Afghan revolution and change in regime had taken place in April 1978, one year before the Iranian revolution and the victory of the Sandinistas in Nicaragua. The new People's Democratic Republic of Afghanistan set about legislating land reform, equality for the diverse ethnic groups, and rights for women and girls in the family and the society. Almost immediately, the United States, Saudi Arabia, Pakistan, Egypt, and other countries formed a coalition in opposition to the pro-Soviet Afghan government. When the Islamist rebellion, backed by the CIA since the summer of 1978, came to threaten the viability of the new republic, the Soviet Union reluctantly agreed to the Afghan government's request that troops be sent to help stabilize the situation. Shortly thereafter, the United States beefed up its covert operation to support the mujahideen (the coalition of Islamist rebels) and end communism in both Afghanistan and the Soviet Union. That women and girls would forfeit schooling, the right to work, and rights in the family under an Islamist regime was of no consequence.[13] Surprisingly, it was of no apparent consequence to international women's groups, either. Feminists in the United States and Europe were silent; they extended no support to Afghan women and did not express any concerns about the implications of American support for Islamists. The silence and confusion of the 1980s may have been due to the anti-communism of liberal feminist groups; to an idealization of "Islamic guerrillas"; to a misplaced cultural relativism; or to confusion and ignorance of Afghanistan. In any event, the left-wing government was defeated in late April 1992, and the mujahideen came to power—only to turn on each other and to bring about a reign of lawlessness and warlordism. It was not until the mid-1990s, after the Taliban had removed the mujahideen from power and instituted a draconian gender regime, that feminists around the world began to take notice and to respond to appeals from Afghan and Pakistani feminists for solidarity and support. Thus began the highly effective international feminist campaign against diplomatic recognition of the Taliban. In the United States, the Feminist Majority led a vocal and visible campaign against "gender apartheid" in Afghanistan.

These and other campaigns were boosted in part by the computer revolution. The new information and computer technologies helped women connect and share information, plan and coordinate activities more rapidly, and mobilize more extensively. Two feminist networks focusing on communications came to serve as conduits of activist materials. These were the International Women's Tribune Center, based in New York, and ISIS International Women's Information and Communication Service, with one center in Quezon City, Philippines, and another in Santiago, Chile. ISIS International produced *Women in Action*, *Women's World*, and other communications. A 2002 issue of *Women in Action* included articles on media (mis)representations of the Afghan crisis and the Israeli–Palestinian conflict, while a 2002 issue of *Women's World* had updates on women in Sierra Leone, the Democratic Republic of Congo, Sudan, Sudanese refugees in Kenya, Burundi, Afghanistan, Pakistan, Albania, India, Kosovo, and Colombia.

As TFNs proliferated in the 1990s, they helped bridge the North–South divide among women activists and transcended the earlier political and ideological differences through the adoption of a broader feminist agenda that included a critique of neoliberalism and structural adjustment policies as well as an insistence on women's full citizenship, reproductive rights, bodily integrity, and autonomy no matter what the cultural context. Eventually, that common agenda took the form of the 1995 Beijing Declaration and Platform for Action. Along the way to Beijing, though, there were other venues where the world's women agreed on issues pertaining to gender justice, notably the UN world conferences of the 1990s—the United Nations Conference on

Environment and Development (UNCED) in Rio de Janeiro in 1992, the Human Rights Conference in Vienna in 1993, the International Conference on Population and Development (ICPD) in Cairo in 1994, and the World Summit for Social Development (the Social Summit) in Copenhagen in 1995. At these conferences, women declared that environmental issues were women's issues, that women's rights were human rights, that governments were expected to guarantee women's reproductive health and rights, and that women's access to productive employment and social protection needed to be expanded. Slowly, new frames emerged that resonated globally and that have come to be adopted by women's groups throughout the world: women's human rights; gender justice; gender equality; ending the feminization of poverty; ending violence against women.

TFN activities as well as partnerships with other advocacy networks resulted in some successes at the UN conferences of the 1990s. TFN lobbying led to the insertion of important items in the final Vienna Declaration of the 1993 Conference on Human Rights, such as the assertion that violence against women was an abuse of human rights, and attention to the harmful effects of certain traditional or customary practices, cultural prejudice, and religious extremisms. The declaration also stated that human rights abuses of women in situations of armed conflict—including systematic rape, sexual slavery, and forced pregnancy—were violations of the fundamental principles of international human rights and humanitarian law. TFNs were influential in lobbying delegates for a favorable Outcome Document at the 1994 ICPD, which included references to women's rights to reproductive health and services. They were active at the March 1995 Social Summit, where they criticized structural adjustment and drew attention to its adverse effects on women and the poor; and, as noted, they were vocal and visible at the September 1995 Beijing conference.

Some scholars have distinguished between professionalized women's lobbying groups (NGOs or INGOs) and "grassroots" women's groups. The former are said to be elitist while the latter are more movement-oriented. This may be an arbitrary distinction, however, because many of the professionalized TFNs are led and staffed by feminist activists with strong commitments to gender equality, women's empowerment, and social transformation. Moreover, the women's movement is diffuse and diverse, with different types of mobilizing structures, discourses, and action repertoires. The overarching frame is that of achieving gender equality and human rights for women and girls. Strategies vary—including grassroots organizing, research and analysis, lobbying efforts, coalition-building, and public protests. All of these means, therefore, are movement-oriented.

Table 4.1. Types of Transnational Feminist Networks

Transnational Feminist Network	Website	Location
Critique of Economic Policy		
Development Alternatives with Women for a New Era (DAWN)	http://www.dawn.org.fj	Fiji
International Women's Tribune Center (IWTC)	http://www.iwtc.org	U.S.
Network Women in Development Europe (WIDE)	http://www.eurosur.org/wide/home.htm	Brussels, etc.
Women's Environment and Development Organization (WEDO)	http://www.wedo.org	New York
Women's International Coalition for Economic Justice (WICEJ)	http://www.wicej.addr.com	U.S.
Advocacy for Women's Human Rights and Anti-fundamentalism		
Arab Women's Solidarity Association (AWSA)	http://www.awsa.net	U.S.
Association for Women's Rights in Development (AWID)	http://www.awid.org	Canada
Center for Women's Global Leadership (CWGL)	http://www.cwgl.rutgers.edu	U.S.
Equality Now	http://www.equalitynow.org	U.S., Kenya
Madre	http://www.madre.org/index.html	U.S.
Sisterhood Is Global Institute (SIGI)	http://www.sigi.org	Canada
Women Living Under Muslim Laws (WLUML)	http://www.wluml.org	Nigeria, Pakistan, U.K.
Women's Caucus for Gender Justice	http://www.iccwomen.org	U.S.
Women's Human Rights Network (WHRNet)	http://www.whrnet.org	n/a
Women's Learning Partnership (WLP)	http://www.learningpartnership.org	U.S.
Women for Women International	www.womenforwomen.org	U.S.
Peace, Anti-militarism, Conflict Resolution		
Association of Women of the Mediterranean Region (AWMR)	http://digilander.libero.it/awmr/int	U.S., Cyprus
Code Pink	www.codepink4peace.org	U.S.
Grandmothers for Peace International	www.grandmothersforpeace.org	U.S.
Madre	www.madre.org	U.S.
Medica Mondiale	http://www.medicamondiale.org/_en/projekte/jugoslawien	Germany
Women for Women International (WWI)	http://www.womenforwomen.org	U.S.
Women in Black	http://balkansnet.org/wib	Various countries
	http://www.womeninblack.net	
Women's International League for Peace and Freedom (WILPF)	http://www.wilpf.org	Switzerland, U.S.

NEOLIBERALISM AND THE WOMAN QUESTION

"The woman question" is the term that was used by socialist, communist, and nationalist movements in the nineteenth and early twentieth centuries to describe both the oppression that women faced in most societies and the alternative vision that the movement offered. I use it here to refer to more recent feminist contentious politics concerning the impacts of neoliberal economic policies on women and the prescribed alternatives.

The latter part of the 1990s saw feminists addressing issues of globalization and the new global trade agenda. Feminist scholar-activists had been highly critical of structural adjustments—with their concomitant policies of privatization and liberalization—and they were now alarmed by the global reach of neoliberalism. A wave of workshops was organized and publications produced to increase knowledge about the technical details of trade liberalization and its gender dynamics. Of concern was that neoliberal policies—with the attendant features of flexible labor markets, privatization of public goods, commercialization of all manner of services, and "free trade"—threatened the economic security of workers, small producers, and local industries; placed a heavy burden on women to compensate for social cutbacks and deteriorating household incomes; and led to increased vulnerability and poverty. TFNs and others argued that the new rules of global free trade undermined existing national laws that protect workers, the environment, and animals; and that WTO intellectual property provisions allowed large corporations to appropriate (through patents) the knowledge and products of Third World countries and their local communities. Additionally, transnational feminists argued that the employment losses and dislocations brought about by the new international trade agreements would be disproportionately borne by women.[14]

TFNs such as DAWN (Development Alternatives with Women for a New Era), WIDE (Network Women in Development Europe), and WEDO (Women's Environment and Development Organization) prepared documents analyzing the policies and activities of multinational corporations, the World Bank, the International Monetary Fund (IMF), the World Trade Organization (WTO), and the policy stances of the U.S. government. They criticized the World Bank and the International Monetary Fund for their corporate bias and for policies that undermined the well-being of workers and the poor, while the WTO was charged with conducting its deliberations in secret and not subjecting them to rules of transparency and accountability. The previously named transnational feminist groups and others joined broad coalitions such as Jubilee 2000 for Third World debt cancellation, which involved labor, religious, environmental, and human rights groups challenging corporate capitalism and global inequalities. As such, transnational feminist groups were allied with, and indeed became part of, the global justice movement as it formed in the late 1990s and into the new millennium. It is important to note, however, that the global feminist agenda on neoliberalism preceded that of the global justice movement by about a decade.[15]

An example of transnational mobilizing around neoliberalism is the World March of Women 2000. The initiative, which had been launched two years earlier in Montreal, Canada, by the Fédération des Femmes du Québec, culminated in a series of coordinated marches and other actions held around the world to protest poverty and violence against women. Nearly 6,000 organizations from 159 countries and territories were represented in the rallies and marches held. It is noteworthy that women activists from countries of the Middle East and especially North Africa, not usually visible in transnational feminist organizing and mobilizing around economic justice, were involved in the planning and execution of the march.[16] Women trade unionists were also involved; for example, in April 2000, some three thousand trade unionists, including many women workers, marched in Durban, South Africa, in an event organized jointly by the International Confederation of Free Trade Unions (ICFTU) and its South African affiliates. The demands included affordable and accessible housing and transportation; protection against all forms of violence; equal rights for women in the workplace and throughout society; an end to structural adjustment programs and cutbacks in social budgets and public services; cancellation of the debt of all Third World countries; making gender issues central to labor policies and programs; and treatment and protection for people with HIV/AIDS.[17]

The initiative's *Advocacy Guide to Women's World Demands* described the world as governed by two forces: neoliberal capitalism and patriarchy, which were singled out as the structural causes of poverty and forms of violence against women:

> We live in a world whose dominant economic system, neo-liberal capitalism, is fundamentally inhuman. It is a system governed by unbridled competition that strives for privatization, liberalization, and deregulation. It is a system entirely driven by the dictates of the market and where full employment of basic human rights ranks below the laws of the marketplace. The result: the crushing social exclusion of large segments of the population, threatening world peace and the future of the planet. . . .

Neoliberalism and patriarchy feed off each other and reinforce each other in order to maintain the vast majority of women in a situation of cultural inferiority, social devaluation, economic marginalization, "invisibility" of their existence and labor, and the marketing and commercialization of their bodies. All these situations closely resemble apartheid.

The World March of Women proposed concrete measures to combat poverty and incidents of violence against women: an end to structural adjustment policies and to cutbacks in social budgets and public services; implementation of the Tobin tax on speculative transactions and for financial justice; and changes to global governance such as the democratization of the United Nations (including the Security Council), and the establishment of a World Council for Economic and Financial Security. These demands were presented to the president of the World Bank on October 15, 2000.[18]

Continuing its activities to this day, the World March of Women remains an important actor within the Global Justice Movement and the World Social Forum. It participated actively in the World Social Forum in Porto Alegre, Brazil, in 2001; was involved in the People's Summit in Quebec in April 2001; was present during the anti–G-8 demonstrations in Genoa, Italy, in July 2001; and was present again in 2002 in Porto Alegre, where the March organized a seminar on feminism and globalization.[19] In 2005 the network launched another global mobilization, its first since 2000, centered on the Women's Global Charter for Humanity. As described by Pascale Dufour and Isabelle Giraud, the run-up to the mobilization entailed compromises on the network's agenda (for example, on language pertaining to abortion and homosexuality) but had the effect of including many more women's groups, especially African and Indian ones. While painful to some members, this decision was important to the goal of building a global social movement with a collective identity.[20]

FUNDAMENTALISM AND THE WOMAN QUESTION

Chapter 3 described the rise of Islamism and the collusion of states, including the United States, in its emergence and growth. Part of the collective action repertoire and framing strategy of Islamist movements was to demand the reinforcement and strengthening of existing Islamic laws and norms, or their introduction and strict application. In addition to the prohibition of alcohol and usury, and the insistence that women veil in public, Islamists insisted on orthodox interpretation and implementation of Muslim family laws, which regulate marriage, divorce, child custody, inheritance, and other aspects of family relations. In particular, Muslim family laws—which date from the Middle Ages and reflect one or another of the four Sunni schools of jurisprudence, and were codified in the modern period of state-building—place females under the authority of male kin and wives under the control of husbands. Although notions of Islamic "complementarity" of sex roles may once have been considered equitable and natural, the rise of second-wave feminism and subsequently of "global feminism" put feminism and fundamentalism on a collision course.

This is the global context in which the international solidarity network Women Living Under Muslim Laws (WLUML) was formed. In July 1984, nine women—from Algeria, Sudan, Morocco, Pakistan, Bangladesh, Iran, Mauritius, and Tanzania—set up an action committee of Women Living Under Muslim Laws in response to "the application of Muslim laws in India, Algeria, and Abu Dhabi that resulted in the violation of women's human rights."[21] By early 1985, the committee had evolved into an international network of information, solidarity, and support, with such key figures as Marieme Hélie-Lucas of Algeria and France, Salma Sobhan of Bangladesh, Ayesha Imam of Nigeria, and Khawar Mumtaz and Farida Shaheed of Pakistan. These and other feminists associated with the network were concerned about changes in family laws in their countries, the rise of fundamentalism and aggressive Islamist movements, and threats to the legal status and social positions of women in Muslim-majority societies.

Other networks of anti-fundamentalist feminists also were formed, by expatriate Iranian women in Europe and the United States, and by South Asian feminists in Britain. Sisterhood Is Global, a network created by the veteran American feminist Robin Morgan, was directed by an expatriate Iranian feminist, Mahnaz Afkhami, during most of the 1990s; under her leadership, SIGI emerged as a highly visible network dedicated to Muslim women's human rights through practical means such as training workshops, conferences, policy dialogues, manuals, and publications. In 2000, Afkhami formed the Women's Learning Partnership for Rights, Development, and Peace (WLP). Dedicated to women's leadership and empowerment, WLP defines itself as "a builder of networks, working with eighteen autonomous and independent partner organizations in the Global South, particularly in Muslim-majority societies, to empower women to transform their families, communities, and societies." The goals are to "improve the effectiveness of feminist movements in Muslim-majority societies and globally" and to help women secure human rights, contribute to the development of their communities, and "ultimately create a more peaceful world."[22]

Returning to WLUML, tasks for the network were established at the first planning meeting, in April 1986, involving ten women from Algeria, Morocco, Tunisia, Egypt, Sudan, Nigeria, India, Pakistan, and Sri Lanka. The tasks were to create international links between women in Muslim countries and communities; to share information on their situations, struggles, and strategies; and to strengthen and reinforce women's initiatives through publications, exchanges, and an Alert for Action system.[23] Since then, WLUML has become a network of women who are active in their local and national movements but who meet periodically to reach a strategic consensus. In 1997, some thirty-five activists from eighteen countries gathered in Dhaka, Bangladesh, to agree on a plan of action. A new plan was adopted in Dakar, Senegal, in January 2006.

Fiercely anti-fundamentalist since its inception, WLUML began to issue warnings as early as 1990 about an "Islamist international" with the organizational, human, financial, and military means to threaten secularists, feminists, and democrats.[24] In recent years, because of the FIS and GIA record of terrorism, including harassment, kidnapping, rape, and murder of Algerian women, WLUML has opposed any legalization of these groups without prosecution of those responsible for crimes, and has protested the granting of political asylum in the West to individuals associated with these organizations.[25]

As a fluid group rather than a membership-based organization, WLUML gives priority to creating strong networks and ties of solidarity among women across countries rather than seeking to influence national or global policy through interaction with governments or inter-governmental bodies. Nonetheless, it was present at the United Nations' world conference on human rights, held in Vienna in 1993, and sponsored the participation of Khalida Messaoudi, an Algerian feminist leader.[26] WLUML also took part at the 1994 UN conference on population and development, where it joined other feminist networks in criticizing efforts by the Vatican, conservative states, and Christian and Muslim fundamentalists to remove references to women's reproductive rights in the conference declaration. These conferences helped WLUML to expand its collaborations and alliances with transnational feminist networks such as WIDE and DAWN—in addition to its ongoing links with the Center for Women's Global Leadership at Rutgers University, Shirkat Gah in Lahore, Pakistan, and Baobob in Lagos, Nigeria.

WLUML's collective action repertoire includes gathering and disseminating information on formal and customary laws in the Muslim world, as well as on women's struggles and strategies. Common projects are identified by women in the network and reflect their diverse concerns. A ten-year project on reinterpreting the Quran culminated in a book and increased awareness of the religious women involved in the misapplication of Islamic law in the Muslim world. Particularly active in this project was the Malaysian women's group Sisters in Islam.

The central activity of the network, however, may be identified as its solidarity and support work. WLUML receives appeals and responds to as well as initiates campaigns pertaining to violations of human rights, including women's human rights.[27] In keeping with its focus on monitoring the human rights of women in Muslim countries, extending solidarity, and raising international awareness, WLUML has issued numerous Action Alerts. These have been disseminated by the international coordination office in Europe, the Asia office in Pakistan, and the Africa and Middle East office in Nigeria (now in Dakar). Another activity is documenting and disseminating information in the form of dossiers, or occasional journals, which describe the situation of Muslim women and legal codes in various countries, and which report on the activities of women's organizations. The Asia coordination office, and specifically the women's resource center Shirkat Gah, produces the news sheet. In the late 1990s, many articles were devoted to describing the plight of women in Algeria and in Afghanistan.

Indeed, after the Taliban took control of Afghanistan in September 1996 and instituted a harsh gender regime, WLUML helped disseminate appeals from expatriate Afghan women in Pakistan for international solidarity and support. Feminists throughout the world brought pressure to bear on their governments not to recognize the Taliban, and as a result, only three governments—those of Pakistan, Saudi Arabia, and the United Arab Emirates—came to recognize the Taliban regime. But WLUML was also critical of the U.S. bombing raids in Afghanistan, which the United States conducted following the tragedy of September 11, 2001, in order to bring down the perpetrators, identified as Osama bin Laden, his al-Qaeda network, and their Taliban hosts. WLUML was concerned that the raids brought devastation to ordinary Afghans. And the network accused Western countries of having turned a blind eye to Islamists—and in the case of the United States, having actively supported them. An article in a WLUML newsletter declared:

> Western governments are the prime responsible ones for the creation of these big and small monsters that they are now attempting to fight against.

The West never cared when the Taliban attacked Afghan women's rights, when they assaulted them, when they killed them. It has looked in the other direction while in Algeria the radical Islamic groups have kidnapped, raped, killed and ripped to pieces scores of women—the latest aggression taking place barely two months ago—while in Bangladesh many women have to live with their faces scarred by the acid thrown in their faces by fundamentalists.

And now. Is an end to western hypocrisy going to come with the resounding measures being taken against the terrorism of the radical Islamic networks? Will they be compatible with measures of justice? It does not seem just to carpet-bomb a people, the Afghan people, who in the last years have been the prime victim of a regime which has been indirectly tolerated and harbored. There must be another way of achieving justice.[28]

Exemplifying the fluid and flexible nature of contemporary transnational social movements and their organizations, WLUML's work is maintained through the activities of "networkers" who communicate largely via the Internet but meet occasionally to agree on plans. The January 2006 meeting in Dakar that produced the most recent plan of action was attended by fifty networkers from twenty-two countries, but input was received by affiliates via e-mail. This double strategy of real and virtual communication enabled the network to agree on four priority issues: "peace-building and resisting the impact of militarization; preserving multiple identities and exposing fundamentalisms; widening debate about women's bodily autonomy; and promoting and protecting women's equality under laws."[29] Long engaged in virtual activism, WLUML wages numerous e-campaigns for women's human rights. The network has issued numerous appeals on behalf of Iraqi women; it was the prime vehicle through which information was distributed worldwide in 2005 concerning the planned establishment of a sharia court in Ontario, Canada; and it has initiated or disseminated numerous petitions to protest violations of women's rights. WLUML has worked with other feminist networks and web-based projects—such as the Women's Human Rights Net, a project of the Canada-based Association for Women's Rights in Development—to highlight women's human rights violations as well as examples of feminist collective action. Its website lists seventy-five linked networks, many of them in Middle Eastern or Muslim countries.[30] In all these ways, WLUML links dispersed communities, creating a new cyber-culture and reinforcing a collective identity. Mobilization to protest gender injustices occurs rapidly and often effectively.

Through its virtual activism, therefore, WLUML exemplifies at least two key characteristics of social movement networks in an era of globalization: creating or actively participating in the transnational public sphere; and creating and maintaining a collective identity as networkers for women's human rights. These features pertain also to other feminist networks for women's human rights in the Muslim world, notably the Women's Learning Partnership, which conducts training programs and produces manuals, videos, and publications that are disseminated through its partners across the globe, and which also engages in cyber-activism for Muslim women's human rights. In 2007–2008, for example, the Women's Learning Partnership was active in mobilizing international support for Iranian feminists who were subjected to harassment, imprisonment, or prosecution by the authorities of the Islamic Republic of Iran.

CONFLICT, WAR, AND EMPIRE: FEMINIST RESPONSES

Chapter 1 mentioned one of the oldest transnational feminist networks, and indeed, one of the world's oldest peace organizations. The Women's International League for Peace and Freedom (WILPF) was founded in 1915 by 1,300 women activists from Europe and North America opposed to what became known as World War I.[31] Feminists and women's groups have long been involved in peace work, with analyses of the causes and consequences of conflict, methods of conflict resolution and peace building, and conditions necessary for human security.[32] The activities of anti-militarist and human rights groups such as WILPF, Women Strike for Peace (United States), the Women of Greenham Common (United Kingdom), and the Mothers and Grandmothers of the Plaza de Mayo (Argentina) are well known, and their legacy lies in ongoing efforts to "feminize" or "engender" peace, nuclear disarmament, and human rights. Women's peace activism has been long associated with world affairs.

At the third UN conference on women, which took place in Nairobi in 1985, the themes of Equality–Development–Peace were addressed by attendees in various ways.[33] The Nairobi conference took place in the midst of the crisis of Third World indebtedness and the implementation of austerity policies recommended by the World Bank and the IMF. Feminists were quick to see the links among economic distress, political instability, and violence against women. As the Jamaican scholar-activist Lucille Mathurin Mair noted after Nairobi:

> This [economic] distress exists in a climate of mounting violence and militarism. . . . Violence follows an ideological continuum, starting from the

domestic sphere where it is tolerated, if not positively accepted. It then moves to the public political arena where it is glamorized and even celebrated. . . . Women and children are the prime victims of this cult of aggression.[34]

The era of globalization and a new wave of conflicts brought even more urgency to the matter, spurring the formation of a number of new women-led peace and human rights organizations as well as greater professionalization of networks. It also led to a new international agreement concerning women, peace, and security. The 1990s saw conflicts in Afghanistan, Bosnia, and Central Africa (principally, Rwanda and Burundi), all of which were marked by serious violations of women's human rights. Women's groups responded by underscoring the specific vulnerability of women and girls during wartime, the pervasive nature of sexual abuse, and the need to include women's groups in peace negotiations. Newly formed feminist peace, human rights, and humanitarian organizations and networks included Women in Black, Medica Mondiale, Women Waging Peace, and Women for Women International. Advocacy networks and scholar-activists produced research to show that women's groups had been effective in peace-building in Northern Ireland as well as in Bosnia and Burundi.

In response to such research, lobbying, and advocacy initiatives, the United Nations Security Council issued a resolution that was embraced by women's groups, if not governments. In March 2000 the UN Security Council, in its Proclamation on International Women's Day, recognized that gender equality is an integral component of peace. In October the council convened a special session to consider the situation of women in armed conflict. On October 31 it passed Resolution 1325, calling on governments—and the Security Council itself—to include women in negotiations and settlements with respect to conflict resolution and peace-building.[35] Key points of the resolution are:

- Increasing the representation of women at all decision-making levels
- Integrating a gender perspective into peacekeeping missions
- Appointing more women as special representatives and envoys of the Secretary-General
- Supporting women's grassroots organizations in their peace initiatives
- Involving women as participants in peace negotiations and agreements

- Ensuring protection of and respect for human rights of women and girls
- Protecting women and girls from gender-based violence
- Integrating a gender perspective into disarmament, demobilization, and reintegration of former combatants.

While Security Council Resolution 1325 was widely hailed as a historic achievement in a domain usually considered off-limits to women and the preserve of men, its impact was unfortunately muted not long afterward, when new conflicts erupted that would sideline the resolution in the name of the "global war on terror."

The aftermath of September 11, 2001, and the invasion of Iraq in 2003 galvanized many women, who rallied to existing peace organizations or built new ones. In India, women's groups joined a coalition called Jang Roko Abhiyan (Anti-war Campaign), which condemned the massacre of American civilians on September 11 but called on the United States to accept responsibility for the fallout from past foreign policies and to refrain from military retaliation in Afghanistan which would very likely cause considerable civilian death and suffering.[36] In Pakistan, women's groups held a protest rally on September 25, 2001, against terrorism, religious fundamentalism, and war. The U.S.-based Feminist Majority issued a very measured statement on September 11 that pointed out the U.S. role in the 1980s in supplying "billions of dollars to fund, train, and arm the mujahideen, which gave rise to the Taliban." The statement continued: "Just as we must not condemn the Afghan people for the acts of terrorists, we also should not condemn Arabs and Muslims, the vast majority of whom do not support this so-called religious fanaticism. This extremism, which has now taken the lives of so many American citizens, Afghans, and others, is not about Islam, but is about the use of violence to achieve a political end."[37] A statement from the Women's Center, Medica Mondiale Kosovo, was especially pertinent:

> We have lived through war. We know what it is like to be attacked, to grieve, and to feel anger. We understand the urge for revenge is strong. And we know that it must not be given in to. We know that a violent response can only bring more violence not justice. Instead, it kills more innocent victims and gives birth to new holy avengers. It begins a new cycle and perpetuates more hate, more insecurity, more fear and ultimately more death amongst civilians. We therefore urge the U.S. and its allies to temper their anger and

to refrain from the folly of sweeping military solutions. Terrorists are not nations. And nations must not act like terrorists.[38]

The invasion of Iraq was preceded by massive anti-war protests across
the globe. In the United States, progressive women's groups and feminist activists refused to side with the Bush administration and took part in street
and media protests. The radical feminist magazine *Off Our Backs* carried an
article by the veteran activist Starhawk, in which she wrote: "Oppression of
women is real, in Muslim societies and non-Muslim societies around the
globe. But women cannot be liberated by the tanks and bombs of those who
are continuing centuries-old policies of exploitation, commandeering resources for themselves, and fomenting prejudice against the culture and
heritage which is also a deep part of a woman's being."[39] A press release issued on March 28, 2003, by the U.S.-based feminist humanitarian group
MADRE described a meeting of women's organizations worldwide (including itself) that gathered at the United Nations and urged the General Assembly to "unite for peace." It added: "This action follows a recent call in
New Delhi made by women's organizations from over thirty-five countries
condemning the Bush administration's war against Iraq and urging the General Assembly to challenge U.S. aggression."[40] The spring 2003 issue of *Ms.*
magazine carried a Special Action Alert entitled "No Time for Despair:
Women Take Action Worldwide," signed by American feminists Robin Morgan, Ellie Smeal, and Gloria Steinem. In it the authors referred to "an elec-
tive war launched against Iraq, where 50 percent of the population is under
age fifteen. Yes, they are oppressed by a brutal dictatorship, but it's also
clear—from polls showing that some 70 percent of Americans oppose
Bush's unilateral action against Iraq—that a majority of us don't trust the
judgment of *our* leader." At the bottom of the statement was a listing of
women's organizations and progressive groups that *Ms.* magazine readers
could contact. Also included was a "National Council of Women's Organizations Statement on War with Iraq," stating in part that "U.S. foreign policy should be driven by human rights, justice, and equality—values that
will decrease the threat of terrorism—and not by corporate interests or the
desire to secure natural resources for U.S. consumption." The issue of *Ms.*
magazine also carried a statement by the author and poet Grace Paley entitled "Why Peace Is (More Than Ever) a Feminist Issue."[41]

Code Pink was formed in 2002 by a group of women who had worked
with each other as well as in other networks. Medea Benjamin co-founded
Global Exchange in 1988 with Kevin Danaher; Jodie Evans had worked for

former California governor Jerry Brown; and Gael Murphy was a long-time public health advisor in Africa and the Caribbean. The group's name is a play on the national security color codes established by the Bush administration in the aftermath of September 11, and Code Pink activists have shown their creativity and innovative style of protest in various ways. Wearing pink costumes and engaging in daring acts of public protest, they have become known for infiltrating congressional meetings, unfurling anti-war banners, shouting anti-war slogans, and badgering members of Congress on their stand on the war, military spending, health care for veterans, and support for Iraqi civilians. One of their innovations is the issuance of "pink slips" to political culprits. In one daring act, a Code Pink activist, her hands painted red, approached Secretary of State Condoleezza Rice on Capitol Hill and accused her of having the blood of the Iraqi people on her hands.[42]

In addition to its strategy of direct action, Code Pink's repertoire includes prompting feminist humanitarianism and international solidarity, as evidenced by visits to Baghdad to demonstrate opposition to war and solidarity with the Iraqi people. Medea Benjamin, Jodie Evans, and Sand Brim travelled to Iraq in February 2003, and another trip was organized in December 2003. In December 2004, Code Pink coordinated the historic Families for Peace delegation to Amman, Jordan, involving the three Code Pink founders and a member of the anti-war group United for Peace and Justice (UFPJ), along with several relatives of fallen American soldiers and families of September 11 victims. According to one report: "In an inspiring act of humanity and generosity, they brought with them $650,000 in medical supplies and other aid for the Fallujah refugees who were forced from their homes when the Americans destroyed their city. Although the American press failed to cover this unprecedented visit, the mission garnered enormous attention from Al-Jazeera, Al-Arabiyya, and Dubai and Iranian television, who witnessed firsthand the depths of American compassion."[43]

Code Pink is linked to other feminist and social justice networks, including the National Organization for Women and United for Peace and Justice. MADRE, Women in Black, Women for Women International, and Code Pink engage in operational activities, information exchange, and solidarity work, as well as direct action to protest government policies or inaction. Networks such as the Women's Initiatives for Gender Justice, Women in Conflict Zones Network, and Women Waging Peace engage in research, lobbying, and networking to ensure that war criminals are brought to justice and that local women's peace groups are recognized.

They also advocate for the International Criminal Court (established in 1999 as the first international war crimes court) and for Security Council Resolution 1325. Six women Nobel Peace Prize winners formed the Nobel Women's Initiative in 2007, and its first international conference focused on women, conflict, peace, and security in the Middle East.[44] In addition to these collective efforts, scholar-activists have penned numerous op-ed pieces, journal articles, and books on wars in Afghanistan and Iraq, tying these to capitalism, militarism, and empire. Zillah Eisenstein's *Against Empire*, for example, is a powerful indictment of neoliberal globalization, imperial arrogance, and racism and a clarion call for a polyversal feminism and humanism.[45] Cynthia Enloe's *Globalization and Militarism* offers a trenchant critique of masculinist international relations, especially in the context of the war against Iraq, while also noting the contributions of women peace-builders across the globe.[46]

GLOBAL FEMINISM AND GLOBAL JUSTICE

The global women's movement and the global justice movement are inter-networked social movements. Many transnational feminist networks are active in the global justice movement and participate regularly in the World Social Forum. In the first Forum (2001) women made up 54 percent of participants but less than 15 percent of the most important panelists in the official Forum program. By the third Forum (2003), two major feminist groups—the World March of Women and the Mercosur Feminist Articulation—were responsible for two of the five thematic areas. At the fourth WSF in Mumbai, feminists were placed in charge of the development of several of the self-organized panels. The feminist dialogues that took place at the fifth WSF focused on three key problems: neoliberal globalization, militarism and war, and fundamentalisms.[47] Clearly there have been improvements in women's representation at the WSF, but many activists feel that feminist issues are not present outside the feminist dialogues and sessions. For example, in a report on the third European Social Forum (held in London, October 14–17, 2004), Amandine Bach of WIDE noted that the main demands were: "stop the war; no to racism; end privatization; for a Europe of peace and social justice," and that gender justice seemed outside the forum's scope.[48] At the Africa Social Forum later that year (held in Lusaka, Zambia, December 10–14, 2004), women were in the minority because, in the words of the authors of a report on the Forum, "the leadership of organizations and movements (i.e., those likely to represent organizations at international forums) are men." Amanda Alexander and Mandisa Mbali, the authors of the report, continued: "Essentially, we know that patriarchy and other forms of dominance are being re-inscribed within our movements for resistance." They cited Shallo Skaba, an Ethiopian coffee worker who had appeared at the Africa Court of Women and complained: "'No one is looking for women's problems. No one considers all that women are doing.'"[49]

Global feminism shares with the global justice movement a common opposition to neoliberalism and militarism and also emphasizes an anti-fundamentalist action frame. In particular, WLUML has been alarmed by what it perceives to be a sympathetic stance toward Islamists on the part of some anti-globalization activists, on the basis of a common opposition to empire and to military occupations in Afghanistan, Iraq, and Palestine. In an appeal issued in February 2005 that was prepared for the World Social Forum in Porto Alegre and discussed at the Feminist Dialogues that immediately preceded the Forum, WLUML decried the beginning of an "unholy alliance between a growing number of anti-globalization activists, human rights activists and progressive people in the West in general with Muslim fundamentalists, and the gradual abandonment of progressive democratic forces from within Muslim countries and communities."

The statement continued:

Disturbed by the discrimination and exclusion that affect people of migrant descent in Europe and North America, progressive forces in the West are keen to denounce racism—and rightly so. But subsequently, they often choose to sacrifice both women and our own internal indigenous democratic progressive opposition forces to fundamentalist theocratic dictatorship, on the altar of anti-racism. Or they censor their expressions of solidarity with us for fear of being accused of racism.

Derailed by neocolonial invasions and wars, progressive forces are prepared to support any opposition to the superpowers. We have already witnessed prominent Left intellectuals and activists publicly share the view that they could not care less if fundamentalist theocratic regimes come to power in Palestine or Iraq, provided that the USA and Israel get booted out. We have witnessed representatives of fundamentalist organizations and their ideologists invited and cheered in Social Fora. We have witnessed prominent feminists defend the "right to veil"—and this sadly reminds us of the defense of the "cultural right" to female genital mutilation, some decades ago.

We call on the democratic movement at large, on the antiglobalization movement gathered in Porto Alegre, and more specifically on the women's movement, to give international visibility and recognition to progressive democratic forces and to the women's movement within it, that oppose the fundamentalist theocratic project. We urge them all to stop supporting fundamentalists as though it were a legitimate response to situations of oppression.[50]

This outcry was prompted by two particular complaints: First, at several anti-war rallies in London, speakers from Muslim groups invited to share the platform began and ended their talks with chants of "Allah-o-Akbar." Second, an invitation to speak at the World Social Forum had been extended to the European Muslim intellectual Tariq Ramadan, who had earlier made statements defending the veil as integral to Islamic identity.[51] Similarly, French feminist Christine Delphy's defense of Muslim women's "right to veil" was considered by WLUML incoherent in the absence of an analysis of the complex context in which (re)veiling occurs. Pointing out that Islamists have no quarrel with capitalism, WLUML appealed to progressives not to sacrifice women's human rights in the name of a broad anti-war and anti-imperialist front.

COLLECTIVE IDENTITIES, CULTURAL FRAMES, AND STRATEGIES

What is it that leads women from across the globe to common frames and mobilizing structures? We can identify material conditions at both the macro and micro levels. At a macro level, adverse economic policies, war, and patriarchal fundamentalisms—all aspects of globalization—affect and disadvantage women in distinct ways. These can have a galvanizing effect, especially when political opportunities and resources are available. The global women's rights agenda promoted by the United Nations can also inspire, motivate, and mobilize women. International agreements such as the Women's Convention and the Beijing Platform for Action are still important mobilizing tools that also legitimate women's rights activism in difficult cultural or political circumstances. At a micro level, women's lived experiences within the family and society, including experiences of marginalization in the labor market and the polity (or the continuing significance of the sexual division of labor), can set the stage for receptivity to mobilizing processes. Such common material conditions and experiences can help create collective identities that are then fostered through sustained activism—even if that activism remains within the confines of the virtual public sphere. Similarly, framing strategies in movements or networks can create or reinforce collective identities.

However, we have seen that transnational feminism remains divided on some issues, notably abortion (as distinct from contraception) and homosexuality. One example was provided earlier in this chapter, in connection with the World March of Women. Indeed, Peruvian feminist Virginia Vargas makes a point of referring to "the diverse and plural feminisms that exist."[52] She notes that although all feminists are opposed to fundamentalism, they differ on reproductive and sexual rights. An example is what she calls "the dialogue of differences" between activists from India and Latin America. Latin American feminists view the right to contraception and abortion as central to female autonomy and bodily integrity, and they fight for their legalization and availability. In India, reproductive rights are recognized in Indian law, but this has not provided women with power or autonomy. Instead, abortion rights have been misused and abused to favor the delivery of sons. For this reason, abortion is not viewed as a priority issue for many Indian feminists. Similarly, at the 2007 World Social Forum in Nairobi, heated arguments took place between representatives of progressive church groups and those supporting abortion and sexual rights.

Will these differences be resolved? Or will they remain, in the interest of maintaining and respecting diversity within global feminism? An advantage of the Internet is that sensitive issues can be discussed in less emotive ways than is sometimes the case with face-to-face encounters. The virtual public sphere can prevent direct observation, experience, and knowledge of others that can assist in overcoming biases and creating new bonds of solidarity. For these reasons, activism will continue to proceed on both fronts—the real and the virtual spheres alike. Differences and diversity, meanwhile, will be recognized and celebrated, or they will be accommodated and absorbed within the segmentary, polycentric, and reticulate nature of the global women's movement. After all, transnationalization is both a function of globalization's opportunity structure and a deliberate strategy to broaden the scope, reach, and representation of a social movement.

What are some of the strategies that transnational feminist networks deploy to achieve their goals? Like other transnational social movement groups, they create, activate, or join global networks to mobilize pressure outside states. TFNs build or take part in coalitions, such as Jubilee 2000; the Coalition to End the Third World Debt; Women's International Coalition for Economic Justice; the Women and Trade Network; 50 Years Is Enough; Women's Eyes on the Bank; and United for Peace and Justice. Since the Battle of Seattle in November 1999, feminist groups have become active players in the global justice movement, taking part in the World Social Forum. And while women's groups have been long identified with peace movements, the new conflicts associated with globalization and American militarism have led to the creation of new transnational feminist peace networks. Working alone or in coalitions, transnational feminist networks mobilize pressure outside states via e-petitions, action alerts, and appeals; acts of civil disobedience; other forms of public protest; and sometimes direct action.

Second, TFNs participate in multilateral and inter-governmental political arenas. They observe and address UN departments such as ECOSOC and bodies such as the Commission on the Status of Women (CSW); and they consult for UN agencies and regional commissions. By taking part in and submitting documents to IGO meetings, and by preparing background papers, briefing papers, and reports, they increase expertise on issues. By lobbying delegates they raise awareness and cultivate supporters. The purpose of such interaction with IGOs is to raise new issues—such as gender and trade, women's human rights, and violence against women in war zones—with a view toward influencing policy.

Third, TFNs act and agitate within states to enhance public awareness and participation. They work with labor and progressive religious groups, the media, and human rights groups on social policy, humanitarian, development, and militarization issues. They link with local partners, take part in local coalitions, and provoke or take part in public protests. And fourth, they network with each other, in a sustained process of inter-networking and Internet-working. In all these ways, their activism spans local, national, regional, and transnational terrains. And in all these ways, too, transnational feminist networks reflect the possibilities inherent within global civil society.

The Internet has allowed transnational feminist networks (and other advocacy networks) to retain flexibility, adaptability, and non-hierarchical features while also ensuring more efficiency in their operations. That is, TFNs are now able to perform optimally without having to become formal or bureaucratic organizations. Avoiding bureaucratization is particularly important to feminists. The network form of feminist organizing suggests a mode of cooperation that may be more conducive to the era of globalization, as well as more consistent with feminist goals of democratic, inclusive, participatory, decentralized and non-hierarchical structures and processes. And the "gift" of the Internet has allowed them to transcend borders, boundaries, and barriers in their collective action against neoliberalism, militarism, and fundamentalisms.

CONCLUSION

In this chapter we have discussed the women's rights movement as a global social movement—albeit one with segmentary, reticulate, and polycentric characteristics—and we have identified key social movement organizations and transnational feminist networks focused on issues of neoliberalism, anti-fundamentalism, women's human rights, and peace. We have seen that there are varieties of global feminist activism: research, advocacy, and lobbying; conferences, seminars, and meetings; solidarity and international networking; progressive humanitarian work; protest and direct action. Framing strategies include the extension of international solidarity; critiques of institutions of global governance, U.S. militarism, and specific actions by states and non-state actors; and recommendations for a women-friendly world. We have seen, too, that global feminists have had to tackle differences within their own movement (for example, on sexuality) as well as with other movements (for example, on the presence of fundamentalists in the GJM). Still, whether they are taking on neoliberal economic policy, women's human rights, or war, there are striking similarities in the way that transnational feminists organize and mobilize—a combination of real and virtual activism resulting from the contradictions of globalization and the persistence of gender inequality.

CHAPTER 5

THE GLOBAL JUSTICE MOVEMENT

The global justice movement has been in formation since at least the late 1990s and has become the subject of many new studies. It is being analyzed as a reaction to neoliberal globalization, an expression of "globalization-from-below," a key element of global civil society, and an exemplar of the transnationalization of collective action. Comprised of NGOs, social movement and civil society organizations, transnational advocacy networks, unions, religious groups, and individual activists opposed to neoliberalism and war, the global justice movement exists in varying degrees of coordination and activism across regions. (See table 5.1.) It is arguably most active in Europe.[1] It convenes at the annual World Social Forum, regional forums, and on the web; it plans and coordinates activities; and it takes part in various forms of public engagement to spread its ideas and recruit new supporters. Its campaigns include debt relief or cancellation as well as ending poverty in developing countries; taxing of financial speculations and movements; fair trade and labor rights; environmental protection; and reform or transformation of institutions of global governance.

The existence of the global justice movement, known as "the movement of movements," confirms that issues of class, inequality, and redistribution do not belong to a bygone era. Some have counterposed the so-called old social movements of class-based mobilizations and economic demands to the more recent "new social movements," which focus on identity and lifestyle. In fact, the global justice movement is the inevitable result of the capitalistic features of the contemporary world-system and its attendant globalization processes. And while advocacy and lobbying certainly are part of the collective action repertoire of the movement, some activists are also highly likely to engage in direct action against what they see as the symbols of neoliberal capitalism.

This chapter describes the participants of the GJM, their organizations, leading figures, grievances and critiques, actions and strategies, and proposed alternatives. But first it examines the origins and antecedents of this movement. Although the Battle of Seattle in late 1999 is usually cited as the movement's "take-off," and much of the literature notes the cycle of protests against neoliberalism that ensued throughout Europe and, to a lesser degree, North America, the movement's origins lie in an earlier cycle of protests that took place in the Third World against structural adjustment policies. The literature on globalization and its discontents sometimes overlooks the structural adjustment episode and the anti-IMF riots, but it should be noted that the structural adjustment policies of the 1980s and the trade agenda of the 1990s were part and parcel of the same global trend of neoliberalism capitalism. Indeed, many of the older participants of today's global justice movement were involved in various protests against structural adjustments in the 1980s. Many also were active in solidarity movements for Central America, South Africa, and Palestine. Thus in recognizing the links between structural adjustments and the new trade agenda, we also should note the two cycles of collective action, one of which took place largely in the Global South. While media reports tend to focus on dramatic protests in Europe and North America, we should recognize the genuinely global nature of the movement for economic justice and its strong roots in the developing world, especially Brazil, where the World Social Forum, a key institution of the global justice movement, was born.

Table 5.1. The Global Justice Movement: Issues and Types of Movements and Networks

Type of Movement or Network	Name	Activities and Frames
Environmental	Greenpeace; Earth First!; Friends of the Earth International	Environmental protection and sustainable development
Indigenous Rights	Congreso Nacional Indígena de México; Confederación de Nacionalidades Indígenas del Ecuador; Zapatistas	For cultural and land rights
Feminist	DAWN; Marche Mondiale des femmes; WLUML; WIDE; Feminist Articulation Mercosur	Feminist Dialogues; gender justice; women's human rights
Human Rights	Amnesty International; Fédération international de droits humains; Students Against Sweatshops; Global Exchange	For civil, political, and socio-economic rights of citizens and immigrants
Labor	Australian Council of Trade Unions; Canadian Labour Congress; COSATU; Korean Confederation of Trade Unions	Worker and trade union rights; against job loss and outsourcing; worker solidarity
Anti-poverty	Oxfam; Jubilee South; Make Poverty History	Against neoliberalism; for sustainable development; end Third World debt
Peace	Peace Boat; Code Pink; WILPF; Stop the War Coalition; United for Peace and Justice	Against militarism and war; creating sustainable peace
Religious	Christian Aid; World Council of Churches; Catholic Agency for Overseas Development	Support for the poor; abolish the debt; critique of neoliberalism
Third Worldist	Focus on the Global South; Third World Network; Third World Forum	Against neoliberalism and imperialism; for deglobalization and local/regional solutions
Anti-corporate governance	50 Years Is Enough!; ATTAC; Public Citizen	Democratize global governance; tax financial markets

Notes: Some of these organizations and networks are or have been on the International Council of the World Social Forum. Also, some are involved in two or more movements.

FROM STRUCTURAL ADJUSTMENTS AND ANTI-IMF RIOTS TO THE GLOBAL TRADE AGENDA AND ANTI-WTO PROTESTS

Structural adjustment policies (SAPs) were first implemented in some African and Latin American countries as a result of the debt crisis in the 1970s and early 1980s. The policy changes were conditions for receiving new loans from the IMF or World Bank, or for acquiring lower interest rates on existing loans. The conditions were implemented to ensure that the money lent would be spent in agreement with the general goals of the loan. The policies aimed to balance budgets and increase competitiveness through trade and price liberalization. Some of the conditions for structural adjustment included cutting social expenditures (also known as austerity), devaluation of currencies, trade liberalization, balancing budgets and not overspending, removing price controls and state subsidies, and improving governance and fighting corruption. By the late 1980s, some seventy countries of the Global South had submitted to the World Bank and IMF programs. Economist Lance Taylor and his associates, among others, documented the difficulties of economic reform.[2]

SAPs came to be criticized by activists for halting development, exacerbating poverty, or creating new categories of the poor. Debt servicing and balanced budgets required austerity measures that led governments to halt development planning, cut back on social spending, or seek "cost recovery" through the implementation of "user fees" in sectors such as health and education, as well as through the elimination of subsidies for utilities and basic foodstuff. Other measures such as foreign exchange restructuring and contraction of the public sector wage bill resulted in a reduction of real wages, rising unemployment, and deteriorating living standards. As one activist noted, "Ghana is supposed to be one of the Bank's success stories, but in the 1990s, the Bank itself calculated that it would take the average Ghanaian forty years to regain the standard of living she had had in the 1970s."[3] Scholar-activist Walden Bello of the Philippines interpreted structural adjustment not only as a way of instituting market discipline but also as a way of disciplining the Third World and imposing a single economic model, that of global neoliberal capitalism. Among the milestones he identifies in the process of institutionalizing neoliberalism are "the IMF's new role as the watchdog of the Third World countries' external economic relations in the 1970s; the universalization of structural adjustment in the 1980s; and the unilaterialist trade campaign waged against the Asian 'tiger economies' by Washington beginning in the early 1980s."[4]

When highly indebted Third World countries followed the policy advice of traveling World Bank and IMF economists without consulting trade unions or civil society organizations, and when households began to feel the financial pinch, popular protest was inevitable. A cycle of protests—which at the time were called food riots or anti-IMF riots—enveloped the Third World from the latter part of the 1970s, when the first structural adjustment policies were introduced, to the early 1990s. This pattern of public grievances is illustrated in table 5.2.

David Seddon and John Walton's analysis of structural adjustments and their listing of the anti-IMF riots show that Mexico experienced two such riots in 1986. Some years later, Mexico entered into discussions with the United States and Canada to form a regional free trade agreement that would ostensibly improve economic relations through the freer flow of capital and goods. Thus was born the North American Free Trade Agreement, or NAFTA. Very quickly it came to be seen as a joint corporate-state strategy that had eschewed consultation with unions and civil society groups. It was also viewed as a plan that would best serve the interests of American corporations rather than workers, and therefore protests arose from those on the left in all three countries.

The critique of NAFTA coincided with the emergence of the Zapatista movement. Its dramatic appearance in early 1994—on the day that Mexico officially adopted NAFTA—captured the imagination of leftists and globalization critics everywhere. With the charismatic Subcomandante Marcos as its chief spokesperson, the Zapatista Army of National Liberation (its Spanish acronym is EZLN) arose from the longstanding indigenous movement but was also a direct response and reaction to Mexico's adoption of NAFTA. As Marcos observed in an interview, "The economic system is not on the table for discussion," meaning that the "dialogue" proposed by the government of Vicente Fox would not include a rethinking of the country's neoliberal economic policy path. The solution, therefore, was a movement strategy at once innovative (as in the notion of "constructing a table" at which to sit with the government and engage in dialogue) and traditional (including an armed force).[5]

The decade also saw powerful international campaigns to cancel the Third World debt, establish fair trade with developing countries, and oppose the spread of genetically modified food by major corporations. These initiatives were framed in the language of development, morality, ethics, and justice, and brought to international prominence advocacy groups such as Food First, Oxfam, and Greenpeace. Indeed, Greenpeace was one

Table 5.2.   Number of Protests against Structural Adjustment, by Country and Date

Country	Date of First Protest	Number
Peru	July 1976	14
Egypt	January 1977	1
Ghana	September 1978	1
Jamaica	January 1979	3
Liberia	April 1979	1
Philippines	February 1980	4
Zaire	May 1980	4
Turkey	July 1980	1
Morocco	June 1981	3
Sierra Leone	August 1981	2
Sudan	January 1982	3
Argentina	March 1982	11
Ecuador	October 1982	5
Chile	October 1982	7
Bolivia	March 1983	13
Brazil	April 1983	11
Panama	October 1983	2
Tunisia	January 1984	1
Dominican Republic	April 1984	3
Haiti	May 1985	6
El Salvador	May 1985	4
Costa Rica	May 1985	2
Guatemala	September 1985	1
Mexico	February 1986	2
Yugoslavia	November 1986	7
Zambia	December 1986	2
Poland	March 1987	6
Algeria	November 1987	3
Romania	November 1987	3
Nigeria	April 1988	2
Hungary	August 1988	2
Venezuela	February 1989	7
Jordan	April 1989	1
Ivory Coast	February 1990	1
Niger	February 1990	1
Iran	August 1991	1
Albania	February 1992	1
India	February 1992	3
Nepal	April 1992	1

Source: Walton and Seddon 1994.

of the founding members of the 50 Years Is Enough network, which launched a campaign in 1994 to call for an end to the World Bank and the IMF on the basis of their failed policies in the developing world. Other groups involved in the network were the Development Group for Alternative Policies (D-Gap), the International Rivers Network, Global Exchange, Friends of the Earth, the Maryknoll Office for Global Concerns, and the United Methodist Women's Division.[6]

In the latter part of the 1990s, the anti-debt campaign collected millions of signatures and held successful mass actions involving tens of thousands of people. Called Jubilee 2000, the campaign took its name from the biblical notion of Jubilee, or periodic forgiveness of debts, and attracted many progressive religious persons. A powerful coalition of left-wing and religious groups, its objective was to cultivate international concern and mobilization for the elimination of Third World debt. In 1998, when leaders of the core countries met in Birmingham, England, at the invitation of British Prime Minister Tony Blair, some seventy thousand activists congregated to form a human chain ("make a chain to break the chains of debt") to tell the G-7 summit that it had to act on debt cancellation.[7] The campaign proved highly influential and effective, and politicians agreed to cancel billion of dollars worth of debt for forty-two developing countries.[8]

In the United States, activists for labor rights launched campaigns to draw national and international attention to sweatshop conditions in the global commodity chains that were producing cheap goods for retail enterprises such as Nike, the Gap, and Wal-Mart. The campaign drew students on college campuses across the U.S., and protest actions in front of the local Wal-Mart store became a staple of college towns.

In Europe, Asia, and Canada, concern began to grow over the new rules and regulations attached to the emerging world trade regime. Activists were alarmed by the creeping commercialization—through privatization and patents—of all manner of services, natural resources, and traditional knowledge. Other concerns were the future of biodiversity and the safety of genetically modified foods, which were being promoted by multinational agribusinesses and some governments.

Another major campaign in the late 1990s was the worldwide opposition to the Multilateral Agreement on Investment (MAI). From 1995, the MAI was being negotiated in secret at the OECD in Paris, and was tied to what activists later would call "the new global trade agenda" led by the World Trade Organization (WTO). The MAI would have enabled governments to hasten trade agreements, and it would have given huge advantages to transnational corporations, allowing them the right to sue governments for introducing measures that might limit their present or even future profits.[9] The U.S. administration of president Bill Clinton was in favor of such a fast-track negotiating authority, but the proposed MAI came to the attention of activists. Activists in the Global South raised the alarm, and in the U.S., leading roles in the anti-MAI coalition were played by Ralph Nader, Lori Wallach, and others within the Washington-based advocacy association Public Citizen. After the details of the secret agreement became public across Europe and North America, the bad publicity came to worry politicians in France, whose ruling coalition of Socialists, Communists, and Greens decided to withdraw from the MAI negotiations. This disruption effectively killed the MAI, which was considered a major victory for the emerging global justice movement.

In the Global South, the policies of structural adjustment were being succeeded by the full transition from the former model of state-directed economic development with large public sectors, high government spending, and protection of domestic industries to a neoliberal model of denationalization, privatization, and liberalization of prices and trade. The shift to free markets, however, was not smooth, as market volatility created regional macroeconomic crises in Latin America and Southeast Asia. Mexico and Argentina were especially hard-hit in the mid-1990s, but working people throughout the two regions experienced declining labor earnings, rising unemployment, and inflation.[10]

Concern over global developments and the social implications of the neoliberal economic policy turn set the stage for the now famous Battle of Seattle. In late November 1999, the WTO's Ministerial Conference was scheduled to hold a millennial round of world trade negotiations in Seattle, a coastal city in the U.S. state of Washington that was home to the Boeing Corporation and Microsoft. There, some thirty thousand militants blocked the delegates' entry to the conference. The Battle of Seattle has become a watershed event in the history of the global justice movement, and is widely seen as the precipitating act. It was followed by a cycle of protests against the WTO, the World Bank, the IMF, and the the G-8. Although there was a brief lull in the protests following the attacks of September 11, 2001, the actions against neoliberal capitalism continued, and expanded into work against the invasion and occupation of Iraq and U.S. plans for the privatization and sale of Iraqi economic assets and natural resources, including its oil industry. What is more, the mobilizations assumed an increasingly coordinated nature, culminating in the creation of a new global activist institution, the World Social Forum, which first convened in Porto Alegre, Brazil, a stronghold of the left-wing Workers' Party, in 2001.

TRANSNATIONAL OPPORTUNITIES

The preceding narrative of movement activity and emphases—from sporadic, nationally based structural adjustment protests and "food riots" to highly coordinated trade and anti-globalization demonstrations—helps us to understand the links between global economic restructuring and collective action, or how "globalization-from-above" engendered "globalization-from-below." Still, such discussion raises questions about how and why global mobilizations were able to emerge when they did. To better explain the rise of the global justice movement and its new institution, the World Social Forum, we return to social movement theory and examine the political opportunities that were available to movement activists. In particular, we identify three transnational opportunities that were conducive to the emergence and expansion of the new mobilizing structures: the spread and increasing use of the Internet; the UN conferences of the 1990s; and the coming to power of the Workers' Party in Brazil. That these events should have occurred at the same time that neoconservative intellectuals were touting the "end of history" and a world future of liberal democracy and capitalism captures the ironies and paradoxes of history.

The end of the Cold War coincided with the spread of new information and communications technologies, and together these developments offered opportunities for cross-border meetings, organizing, and mobilizing. Travel across borders that were once difficult to traverse became easier as well as cheaper, while the Internet made communications faster and more expansive. Personal computers were now cheaper to buy, making the use of e-mail an increasingly common form of communication. The Internet allowed for the formation of numerous websites that became increasingly interactive; they were important sources of information and exchange as well as highly effective mobilizing tools for the planning of "global days of action." Movement media such as Indymedia captured various protests on film, issuing videos that were shown on campuses and at community meetings in North America, helping to recruit more people to the emerging global justice movement. Scholars have studied the implications of Internet-based mobilizations, or "cyber-activism," not only in terms of recruitment but also in terms of the creation of a "virtual civil society," a "transnational public sphere," and indeed "cyber-democracy."[11]

The United Nations held a series of world conferences in the 1990s, beginning with UNCED in 1991, and activist groups were able to network at the parallel NGO forums. (See table 5.3.) The UN meetings in particular offered political space for the discussion of proposals such as the Tobin tax, while the many conventions, standards, and norms associated with UN conferences provided moral legitimacy to the movement's call for the globalization of rights.[12] We can regard the occurrence of UN meetings in the 1990s as the making of a transnational political opportunity structure conducive to the growth of all manner of non-governmental organizations, activist groups, and transnational advocacy networks. At the UN conferences, activists could lobby delegates and policy-makers, disseminate their publications, and interact with each other.

In the 1990s, therefore, global developments provided an impetus for concerted and collective action. Both symbolic and material resources became available to groups critical of the growing power of multinational corporations, international financial institutions, and the neoliberal economic policy agenda. Scholar-activists not only in Europe and North America but also in India, the Philippines, Malaysia, Brazil, and sub-Saharan Africa mobilized their own resources to form or join networks critical of creeping globalization. These included Focus on the Global South, Environnement et Développement du Tiers-monde (ENDA), and the Third World Network, formed by activists from the Philippines, Malaysia, Thailand, Senegal, and India. In some regions, opposition to the presence of the U.S. military was also on the agenda. Regional activism in Southeast Asia helped shut down American military bases in the Philippines in the early 1990s.[13]

A third important opportunity came in the form of the October 2002 Brazilian elections that saw the formation of a left-wing government headed by President Luiz Ignacio "Lula" da Silva of the Workers' Party (PT). The city of Porto Alegre had become the stronghold of the PT, and movement activists were invited there to strategize and plan activities. In 2001 the city played host to the first World Social Forum (WSF), planned explicitly as the counter-conference to the World Economic Forum, held in Davos, Switzerland and attended by world politicians, policy-makers, and corporate heads. As Bello observed, "What the Brazilians were proposing was a safe space where people in the movement could come together to affirm their solidarity."[14] The election of President Lula in November 2002 proved to be especially fortuitous to the global justice movement's resource mobilization and the WSF: the PT has continued to lend moral and financial support to this important transnational institution.

Table 5.3. UN Conferences of the 1990s: Transnational Opportunities for Mobilizations and Framings

UN Conference	Inter-governmental Conference Themes	NGO/Activist Frames
Conference on Environment and Development (Rio de Janeiro, June 1992)	Environmental protection; poverty and environmental degradation; sustainable development	The "plunder of nature and knowledge"; protecting biodiversity; ending privatization and commercialization of "the commons"; reducing pollution, CO_2 emissions, and waste
World Conference on Human Rights (Vienna, June 1993)	Status of human rights conventions and practice in the world	Human rights; indigenous people's rights; "women's rights are human rights"
International Conference on Population and Development (Cairo, September 1994)	Population growth, family planning	Toward reproductive health and rights for women
World Summit on Social Development (Copenhagen, March 1995)	Poverty alleviation, employment generation, tackling social exclusion	Promoting welfare; financing development through the Tobin tax; against structural adjustment and Third World debt
Fourth World Conference on Women (Beijing, September 1995)	Addressing twelve critical areas of concern regarding women and girls	Political and economic empowerment; gender equality; human rights for women and girls

THE GLOBAL JUSTICE MOVEMENT'S
CYCLE OF PROTESTS

Documenting the growth of mobilizations across the globe is a key research strategy of scholars of transnational social movements. Italian scholars Pianta and Marchetti, among others, have tracked the growth of global civil society events and show a steady and rapid increase after 1998. These included protests against the U.S. war and occupation of Iraq on 15 February 2003, 20 March 2004, 19 March 2005, and 18 March 2006.[15] U.S. sociologist Bruce Podobnik has carried out "events analysis" to examine the global spread and sustained nature of protests between 1998 and 2004, as well as the number of protesters at each event. He also has grouped the protests in terms of five categories of "summit events": WTO ministerials; IMF/World Bank annual meetings; G-8 summits; World Economic Forums; and World Social Forums.[16] Faculty and students of world-system theory from the University of California at Riverside have focused on numbers of participants and activities at the World Social Forum, where they have also distributed surveys to capture some key characteristics of movement participants.

In short, the next major mobilizations after the Battle of Seattle took place in Bangkok in February 2000, when a thousand activists marched on a UN trade conference calling for radical changes to the global financial system, which they claimed kept a majority of the world in poverty. This event was followed by the UN Millennium Forum of NGOs in New York in May 2000, with 1,350 representatives of more than 1,000 NGOs. The cycle of protests continued through most of 2000 and 2001, and included the anti-capitalist protests in London on May Day 2000, the anti-globalization protests in Melbourne and Prague in September 2000 and in Montreal the following month, and protests in Zurich in January 2001. When the World Economic Forum met at Davos in February 2001, protests took place there, too. The cycle of protests continued in Quebec City, Canada in April 2001, in Goteborg, Sweden in June during the EU summit, and the following month in Genoa, Italy, where the G-8 were meeting. The demonstrators in Genoa numbered three hundred thousand. In Genoa the police turned nasty; one protester was killed and dozens were hospitalized, while many activists were taken into custody after the police raids. The tragedy of September 11 put a temporary halt to the anti-globalization protests, especially in the United States, but they resumed in early 2002. In February 2002 the World Economic Forum met in New York, and about one thousand anti-globalization protesters appeared. That same month in Italy, fully three million people came out to protest a new labor law. In March, as the European Union summit took place in Spain, about five hundred thousand people held an anti-capitalist protest in Barcelona.[17]

The year 2002 saw increasing activism on war and peace issues, which intensified after the decision by the governments of U.S. president George W. Bush and U.K. prime minister Tony Blair to invade Iraq. In addition to protesting neoliberal capitalism, the Barcelona activists gathered in March denounced Israeli actions in Palestine and U.S. plans to invade Iraq. The anti-globalization movement joined forces with the growing anti-war movement, culminating in a huge demonstration in Florence, Italy, in November 2002, where over a half-million people from all over Europe gathered to protest capitalism and war-making. The start of 2003 saw demonstrations across the globe against the impending invasion of Iraq. On February 15, millions of people around the world joined in huge protests against the imminent war. Anti-war demonstrations in London and Washington, D.C., also took place, led in part by activists from the global justice movement. And when the leaders of the main core countries, the G-8, met in Evian, France, in early June 2003, an alternative summit, along with protests, took place in nearby Geneva, Switzerland.[18] After the 2003 invasion and occupation of Iraq by U.S. and U.K. forces, global protests increasingly took on an anti-war frame. As recently as November 2007, activists from the No Bases Initiative in the Czech Republic staged protests against the plans of the Czech government to host the radar for a U.S. anti-missile system. Throughout this period, participation at the World Social Forum grew significantly after its first meeting in 2001. (See table 5.4.)

As Pianta and Marchetti have aptly observed, "at the turn of the millennium, a structural scale shift occurred in the nature, identities, repertoires of actions, and strategies of global social movements."[19] The Battle of Seattle symbolized a radical challenge to neoliberal globalization and precipitated a cycle of protests, but this impetus converged with other factors, such as the coming to power of the Workers' Party in Brazil, to help launch the World Social Forum. The scope and scale of transnationalization increased dramatically, with activists sharing information and coordinating actions across borders and continents. Greater transnational cooperation among labor, environmental, feminist, and human rights activists was created through participation in the international conferences organized by the UN, as well as through cross-border labor struggles, transnational lobbying campaigns, and global protest events planned and coordinated through the Internet.

Table 5.4.   Global Justice Movement Protests since the Battle of Seattle

Location	When	What Was Protested
Bangkok	February 2000	UN trade conference
Washington, D.C.	April 2000	IMF/World Bank meeting
New York	September 2000	UN millennium summit
Melbourne	September 2000	World Economic Forum
Prague	September 2000	IMF/World Bank meeting
Quebec	April 2001	FTAA meeting
Genoa	July 2001	G-8 summit
Gothenburg	June 2001	EU summit
Barcelona	March 2002	EU summit
Evian and Geneva	June 2003	G-8 summit
Sheffield, U.K.	June 2005	G-8 summit, poverty
Global	2003–2007	Iraq invasion and war
Prague	November 2007	Planned U.S. bases

Sources: Retrieved October 24, 2007, from Global Policy Forum website: http://www.globalpolicy.org/ngos/
advocacy/protest/archive/htm; http://www.archive.org/details/quebeccityprotest2001; Pianta and Marchetti 2007; Campaign for Peace and Democracy 2007, http://www.cpdweb.org/statements/1007/stmt.html;
Waddington and King 2007.

MOBILIZING STRUCTURES

The global justice movement is understood to be a "movement of movements," but it is possible to identify mobilizing structures, key institutions,
and public intellectuals. One of the principal institutions to have emerged in
the new millennium is the World Social Forum, coordinated by an International Council. As Virginia Vargas has noted, "the WSF harbors a multiplic-
ity of movements whose common denominator is the struggle against the
catastrophic consequences of neoliberalism. That struggle is their common
ground."[20] In a sense, the WSF mirrors the global justice movement itself,
and a conscious effort was made to include within the International Council
as many associations as possible that reflected the breadth of the global justice movement. The GJM is highly networked, but according to one survey,
the overall structure "shows a multicentric network organized around four
main movements that serve as bridges that link other movements to one another: peace, global justice, human rights, and environmental."[21] Participants are activists, policy experts, students, intellectuals, journalists, and
artists. Campaigns focus on ending poverty in developing countries, the taxing of capital movements, debt relief or cancellation, fair trade, global human
rights, and reform of international intergovernmental organizations.

Italian sociologist della Porta has drawn attention to the crucial role
played by transnational networks in the organization of the global justice

movement. She defines a transnational network as "a permanent coordination among different civil society organizations (and sometimes individuals such as experts), located in several countries, based on a shared frame on at least one specific global issue, and developing joint campaigns and social mobilizations against common targets at the national or supranational levels."[22] This would be an apt definition for the GJM's sustained and coordinated activities, carried out by organizations in both the Global South and the Global North. Well-known networks in the former region include the Third World Network, Focus on the Global South, ENDA, and DAWN. In Europe and North America one finds the Council of Canadians; ATTAC (France, Germany, Sweden, Norway, Italy, and other countries); Globalize Resistance and Christian Aid (United Kingdom); Movimiento de Resistancia Global (Spain); Center of Concern and Public Citizen (United States); and transnational feminist networks such as WIDE, WEDO, and WICEJ. In North America, the movement also includes university-based student groups and left-wing community organizations.[23]

For reasons having to do with the more social democratic nature of its political culture as well as the availability of all manner of resources, Europe has an especially strong presence in the GJM, involving unions, progressive religious groups, the old left and the new left, farmers, environmentalists, and representatives of some political parties (notably Greens and Communists). A brief diversion on ATTAC is instructive of the strength of the global justice movement in Europe, the influence of this particular civil society movement, and its global reach via cyber-activism. ATTAC, "an action-oriented popular education movement," was founded in France in late 1998 and as of 2007 existed in fifty-one countries. The name stands for Association to Tax Financial Transactions to Aid Citizens, and—inspired by the late Professor James Tobin's proposal—its goal is to tax financial markets and transnational corporations in order to redistribute income globally. ATTAC is also against Third World debt and tax havens and demands the complete restructuring of the World Bank, the IMF, and the WTO in order to move toward greater global economic justice.[24] ATTAC does not regard itself as a non-governmental organization but as a movement—one of the key movements within the global justice movement. Its website offers information in four languages—including the recurrent message "the world is not for sale"—and some of its documents are translated into thirteen languages. According to one account, ATTAC's website gets around 4,000,000 connections from 130 countries per month; about 39,000 documents are downloaded every day; and more than 80,000 people are subscribed to ATTAC's weekly e-mail newsletter.[25] Public intellectuals associated with ATTAC—including Bernard Cassen and Susan George—are also prominent in the global justice movement as a whole, as well as in the World Social Forum.

Other public intellectuals associated with the GJM are Arundhati Roy, Vandana Shiva, Naomi Klein, Medea Benjamin, Virginia Vargas, Tariq Ali, Walden Bello, Martin Khor, Samir Amin, Immanuel Wallerstein, José Bové, Kevin Danaher, and George Monbiot. They also play prominent roles in the World Social Forum.

THE WORLD SOCIAL FORUM

The World Social Forum was organized as the popular alternative to the World Economic Forum, which brings together elites to develop global economic policies. Initially supported by the Brazilian Workers' Party (PT) and the Brazilian landless peasant movement, and intended to be a forum for grassroots movements from all over the world, the WSF has been most frequently held in Porto Alegre, Brazil, a traditional stronghold of the PT. The first meeting of the WSF in 2001 reportedly drew 5,000 registered participants from 117 countries, but by the 2005 meeting there were 155,000 registered participants from 135 countries.[26] The first three meetings took place in Porto Alegre, and in 2004 the venue shifted to Mumbai (Bombay, India). It reverted to Porto Alegre in 2005 but in 2006 a "polycentric" WSF took place in three main venues: Bamako (Mali), Caracas (Venezuela), and Karachi (Pakistan). The 2007 meeting took place in Nairobi, Kenya, in an effort to involve more Africans. The plan is that the meeting will return to Porto Alegre every three or four years. In addition to the annual WSF since 2001, hundreds of regional, thematic, and local Social Forums have been organized, mostly within Latin America and Western Europe. Local forums have been slower to develop within the United States, but they have been held in Boston, Milwaukee, Austin, and Raleigh. In June 2007, the first United States Social Forum took place in Atlanta, Georgia.

The size and scale of networks within GJM/WSF is considerable. As Tom Mertes explains, the Brazilian Sem Terre (landless peasant movement) itself counts in its ranks over a third of a million landless families—"and this is not a passive, card-carrying membership but one defined by taking action: risking the wrath of *latifundários* and the state by occupying land. Within this layer there are, again, around twenty thousand activists."[27] Mertes goes on to compare the massive size of the landless peasant movement to the far smaller scale of individual North Atlantic networks. On the other hand, there are numerous, and very active, North Atlantic networks, including unions, progressive religious groups, feminist groups, and an array of left-wing and social justice activists. They have the human, organizational, and financial resources to attend meetings, conferences, and protest events in their own countries and elsewhere.

Social Forums are both institutions—with their own leadership, mission, and structure—and an "open space" where activists from around the world can meet, exchange ideas, participate in cultural events, and coordinate actions. These events are open to all those opposed to neoliberal globalization and militarism, but "exclude groups advocating armed resistance."[28] Research conducted by scholar-activists such as Jackie Smith, Donatella della Porta, Chris Chase-Dunn, Boaventura Santos, and others show that participants are connected with different movements and types of organizations, including local or national groups. Some participants are long-time veterans of transnational organizations and the left.

Alternative values and cultures are on display at the Social Forums. Fair trade, organic farming, environmental protection, and diversity (bio- and cultural) are promoted, along with concepts of equality, justice, and human rights. The products of neoliberalism are opposed: genetically modified foods, sweatshop labor, commercialization, and global capitalist structures. Opposition is mounted through publications, meetings, boycotts, marches, and (at times) direct action. Protest marches are often accompanied by a carnivalesque atmosphere and evidence of individual and collective creativity, including massive puppets, whistles, drums, and costumes. The global justice movement may be angry at neoliberal globalization but it demonstrates creativity, parody, playfulness, and joy.

Who are the participants in the WSF? Christopher Chase-Dunn and his students at the University of California at Riverside launched a research project on the characteristics, political views, and political activity of WSF participants by surveying individuals attending these meetings.[29] Research has found that most participants tend to come from the country or region in which the WSF is located. Thus, from 2001–2005, most participants were from Brazil and the larger Latin American region, followed distantly by participants from Europe and North America.[30] Another survey also reported a preponderance of participants from Brazil and elsewhere in Latin America: Santos found that at the 2003 WSF, fully 86 percent of participants were Brazilians, but this proportion decreased to 80 percent at the 2005 WSF. At the 2005 WSF, the next largest group came from Argentina

(13 percent), followed by the United States (9.5 percent). A significant proportion of participants are youth (15–24 years of age)—42 percent in 2005, most of whom declared themselves to be students. Most WSF participants are highly educated, with at least some years of university education. Still, 22 percent had between zero and twelve years of schooling only.[31] This is suggestive of a not insignificant participation by non-elites, including workers and peasants. At the 2005 WSF in Porto Alegre, Chase-Dunn and his students found that over one-fifth of their respondents were affiliated with a union.[32] While many were members of professional or artists' unions, this outcome does suggest an affinity with the labor movement, and the possibility for more coordinated action between sectors represented within the GJM.

As noted, the International Council of the WSF seeks to be as representative as possible. As of 2006, out of 136 members, 33 percent were from Europe and 28 percent from Latin America and the Caribbean; 12.5 percent from North America; 9.6 percent from Africa; 6.6 percent from Asia; and 2.9 percent from the Middle East (that is, four members).[33] The Council includes representatives of a large number of major trade unions, regional associations, feminist groups, progressive religious groups, progressive media, and an array of civil society organizations. Feminist groups with members on the International Council of the World Social Forum are Mercosur Feminist Articulation, DAWN, FAMES (Forum des femmes africaines pour un monde de l'économie solidaire), FDIF (Fédération démocratique internationale des femmes), International Gender and Trade Network, National Network of Autonomous Women's Groups, Rede Mulher e Habitat (Women and Shelter Network), Women's Global Network for Reproductive Rights, and the World March of Women.[34]

Another active group within the World Social Forum has been the Mothers and Grandmothers of the Plaza de Mayo. This organization was initiated as a human rights group led by Argentine women who had lost children to the military junta's "dirty war" of the 1970s. Their objectives were to gain information on the whereabouts of grandchildren born during their parents' incarceration, and to achieve an end to dictatorship and the military's impunity. Famous throughout the world, they became one of the most studied women's movements in Latin America. Elizabeth Borland describes how their discourses and activism have in recent years encompassed issues related to neoliberalism, such as external debt, hunger, unemployment, and corruption.[35] This kind of frame alignment reflects the capacity of social movement organizations to resonate with diverse audiences; and it shows their recognition that new political realities require new repertoires of collective action.

As demonstrated in the previous chapter, global feminism and global justice share a common frame of challenging neoliberalism and militarism and calling for democratic decision-making at all levels. At the 2002 World Social Forum, the International Gender and Trade Network produced a statement pointing out that "in the current trading system, women have been turned into producers and consumers of traded commodities and are even traded themselves." The document continued:

> In solidarity with our sisters across the globe, we acknowledge that another world will be possible when systems of inequitable power among governments, among institutions, among peoples, and between women and men have been changed to represent the needs of the majority of people and not the market. . . .
>
> IGTN representatives from Africa, Asia, Latin America, the Caribbean and North America here in Porto Alegre are calling for a halt to WTO, FTAA, the Cotonou Agreement and other regional negotiations that are inherently flawed and demand an alternative multilateral trading system that will include the incorporation of a democratic process, corporate accountability, gender and social impact assessments and a commitment to put human rights and social development at the core of all negotiations. Women have much to lose! Today, we women celebrate our power, our partnership and our vision for peace and social justice, and we will continue in the struggle because—ANOTHER WORLD IS POSSIBLE![36]

The beginning of the WSF saw feminist criticisms of under-representation and of the selection process for invited guests. Critiques came from the Mothers and Grandmothers of the Plaza de Mayo, Flora Tristan Feminist Centre of Peru, and the Mercosur Feminist Articulation.[37] At the third WSF (2003), just 26 percent of speakers were women (ten women and twenty-eight men).[38] This was an improvement in women's representation, but sadly there were cases of violence against women in the Youth Camp, where thirty-five thousand young people camped. As a result, a security force was organized, the Brigadas Lilas, and this too became an issue.[39] Hegemonic masculinity seemed to be operating at two levels: at the level of representation of women and feminist issues, and at the level of the security of young women. What could have become a crisis was resolved through dialogue and mechanisms to improve both safety and representation. At the fourth and fifth WSF, feminist groups were put in charge of a number of key sessions. Women's attendance at the WSF has not only remained steady but also grown: about half of all participants are women, and many prominent spokespersons are women, including Arundhati Roy, Vandana Shiva, Virginia Vargas, Naomi Klein, Susan George, and Medea Benjamin.

Boaventura de Sousa Santos is a Portuguese scholar who is also on the Secretariat of the WSF. In a book he authored on the WSF, he describes the institution as "a set of forums—world, thematic, regional, sub-regional, national, municipal and local—that are organized according to the Charter of Principles."[40] The fourteen-point Charter of Principles was drawn up and adopted in 2001, and it emphasizes the free flow of ideas and exchanges. It begins with the following statement:

> The World Social Forum is an open meeting place for reflective thinking, democratic debate of ideas, formulation of proposals, free exchange of experiences and interlinking for effective action, by groups and movements of civil society that are opposed to neoliberalism and to domination of the world by capital and any form of imperialism, and are committed to building a planetary society directed towards fruitful relationships among Humankind and between it and the Earth.[41]

Apart from agreement with the Charter of Principles, what do participants understand about globalization and its alternatives? A survey at the 2003 WSF found that for participants, globalization meant the following: the concentration of wealth that makes the rich richer and the poor poorer (81 percent); the dominion of the world by capital, commanded by the big corporations (75 percent); a new name for imperialism (68 percent). On the question of "the possibility of societies connecting on the planetary scale," responses were polarized: 47 percent totally or partially agreed; 34 percent totally or partially disagreed; and 20 percent were indifferent. Fully 78 percent disagreed with the statement that globalization meant "more opportunities for all, rich and poor." Participants had strong feelings about the means by which "another possible world" could be achieved: through the strengthening of civil society (94 percent); democratization of governments (78 percent); democratization of multilateral organizations (63 percent). As for whether direct action with use of force could help achieve another world, fully 84 percent of respondents totally or partially disagreed.[42]

Many participants see the WSF as an important instrument for the achievement of cohesiveness and more effective strategizing within the GJM. It is argued that movements are more likely to be cohesive when participants share political goals and beliefs, use similar strategies, and are culturally or socially alike. One result of the diversity within the WSF has been the emergence of a number of polarizing debates. A difference of opinion divides those who would like to see the WSF remain broad, inclusive, and fluid, and those who would like to see more deliberate action and a more unified movement.[43] Other sites of disagreement include the issue of socialism or social emancipation (sometimes also framed as reform or revolution); whether to regard the state as enemy or potential ally; whether to focus on local, national, or global struggles; whether to engage in direct action, institutional action, or civil disobedience; and whether to place greater emphasis on the principle of equality or on the principle of respect for difference.[44]

Chase-Dunn and his students identify five general debates:

- Whether to reform existing social structures and global governance institutions or to fundamentally transform them;
- Whether to create more economic growth in order to meet workers' demands for employment and goods or to reduce growth in order to protect the environment;
- Whether upholding international social and labor standards will protect human rights or simply protect Northern workers' interests at the expense of Southern workers' interests;
- Whether to uphold Western values as universal goals, to respect cultural diversity, or to reconstruct universal values in order to acknowledge the experiences of the marginalized;
- Whether to prioritize democratic initiatives at the local, national, or global levels.[45]

This diversity of perspectives is perhaps inevitable, given that WSF participants encompass indigenous groups, trade unionists, leftists, feminists, and Catholics. This diversity parallels the different strands of the GJM that have been identified by Pianta and Marchetti: 1) *reformists*, with the aim of humanizing or civilizing globalization; 2) *radical critics* with a different project for global issues; 3) *alternatives* who self-organize activities outside the mainstream of the state and market spheres, and 4) *resisters* of neoliberal globalization, who strive for a return to local and national spheres of action.[46] These categories may be seen as dividing lines, or as reflections of healthy debates around the common theme of opposition to neoliberal capitalism, imperialism, and war. For Kevin Danaher of Global Exchange, "Inside, outside, we're all on the same side."[47]

FRAMING THE PROBLEM AND
PROPOSING SOLUTIONS

The global justice movement may have a diversity of grievances and critiques, but opposition to neoliberalism is its master frame and the basis for its collective action. We have seen how the critique of neoliberalism evolved from the earlier critique of structural adjustments and from the global shift away from Keynesian economics. Neoliberalism was behind the onerous Third World debt, deteriorating standards of living, and competition, conflict, and war. It was imposed by "globalizers" such as the World Bank, the IMF, multinational corporations, the WTO, and an emerging transnational capitalist class. But whereas Margaret Thatcher had declared that "there is no alternative" to neoliberal globalization, participants of the Social Forums proclaim that "another world is possible." What are the key elements of this "other world," or of the "other globalization" ("altermondialisation")? First and perhaps foremost is the concept of international solidarity and identity construction of global citizenship. While many participants retain national attachments and remain rooted in local and national struggles, they are also highly vested in the broader planetary and human rights concerns. Thus they express strong opposition to the war in Iraq, sympathy with Palestinians and Lebanese victims of Israeli bombings, and concerns about environmental degradation and global climate change. "Another world" would be one without invasions, occupations, or wars; without hunger, poverty, exploitation, or pollution. A second feature concerns GJM activists' focus on global problems and the worldwide political, economic, and cultural environments. Such work entails both analytical research and public engagement and advocacy. Grievances and critiques, and proposed alternatives, may be summarized as follows:

- Against neoliberal globalization and "market fundamentalism" implemented by large corporations, the World Bank, the IMF, the WTO, and the United States
- Against the persistent North–South divide
- Against capital's domination over labor and the environment
- Against war and imperialism
- For economic justice, environmental justice, and gender justice
- For economic, social, and cultural rights, including rights of indigenous peoples and the landless
- For people-oriented sustainable development
- For local and global democracy

- For global solidarities
- For multilateralism and reform of institutions of global governance
- For a new worldwide program of taxation and redistribution[48]

Is another world, then, possible? Susan George of ATTAC is certain that it is, and she offers a set of ten guidelines for how to achieve it. First, activists need to know "what we're talking about." Globalization is not a harmless process of integrating states and markets, she observes, but rather the latest stage of world capitalism and the political framework that it helps to thrive, replete with inequalities. Second, the planet needs to be salvaged. The new world trade order permits corporations to produce, buy, sell, invest, and even patent life forms, across national borders, but it does not require companies to reduce waste, pollution, and environmental destruction. Third, the actors need to be identified. The World Bank and the IMF (which she calls "the Terrible Twins") are responsible for imposing neoliberal restructuring on indebted Third World countries, while the WTO seeks to commercialize not only goods but also all services. Meanwhile, corporations are constantly seeking to lower labor costs, and the system's shift to the primacy of financial markets portends instability and crises. Fourth, it is important to target the right adversaries. In this respect, George identifies various public and private actors on national, regional, international, and planetary (environmental) levels, such as states and their specific policies; employers' associations; regional bodies aligned with the neoliberal agenda; agribusinesses; the "Terrible Twins," the WTO, and various corporations. Fifth, Europe should "win the war within the West." George is clearly among those who view the EU and the European social model as an alternative to the American model of neoliberal capitalism and war-making. But she adds that efforts by the European Commission and other regional bodies to take the neoliberal route must continue to be resisted.

Sixth, the movement must include everyone and forge alliances. In her book, she goes on to discuss, in nuts-and-bolts terms, how to attract, recruit, and retain activists; and how to forge alliances with progressive faith-based groups, peace groups, and political parties. Seventh, activists must combine knowledge and politics. She cites the example of the anti-MAI campaign, noting that the highly technical aspects of the secretive agreement had to be understood by activists and disseminated in ways that could resonate with a broader public. Eighth, educators must educate. Here she notes the important role of "scholar-activists," or the many academics and "professional knowledge workers" involved in the GJM, and the ways that academics can advance "critical globalization studies."[49] Ninth, George argues for the abandonment of cherished illusions. Here she warns NGOs against accepting corporate-initiated "dialogues" without setting clear objectives and conditions; and she notes the limits of individual lifestyle and consumption changes when compared with larger and sustained collective action such as boycotts. Finally, she insists that the movement continue to practice non-violence. George distinguishes between "Boston tea party–type actions" and violence that results in injury or death. Non-violence, she maintains, distinguishes the GJM from "the violence of the strong, the powerful, and the state." She also notes that activist recourse to violence is counter-productive, as the media tend to exaggerate it, causing it to eclipse other aspects of the movement or campaign.[50]

Other sets of proposals for overcoming neoliberal globalization and creating an alternative world have been issued from within the GJM. The manifesto of Porto Alegre, produced and signed by a number of prominent scholar-activists at the 2005 WSF, proposed twelve ways to make another world possible. The first set of proposals pertained to economic measures, such as cancelling all debts in the Global South; establishing a tax on financial transactions; removing tax and bank account havens; ensuring that all citizens enjoy social security and pensions; promoting fair trade; ensuring food security and sovereignty; and prohibiting every form of patenting knowledge. Another group of recommendations had to do with promoting "cooperative life" in peace and justice, including combating all forms of discrimination and xenophobia; ending the destruction of the environment; and closing down military bases in foreign countries. The last set of proposals, on local and global democracy, called for the right to the free flow of communication and information; and reforming and democratizing international organizations.[51]

Some activists and prominent figures within the GJM prefer "deglobalization" and a focus on local communities. In 2001, the International Forum on Globalization issued a statement on "Alternatives to Economic Globalization" and proposed eight principles, which are summarized here: 1) a new democracy and popular sovereignty; 2) subsidiarity: favoring the local; 3) ecological sustainability; 4) human rights; 5) jobs, livelihood, employment; 6) food security and food safety; 7) equity; 8) cultural, biological, economic, and social diversity.[52] Two of the signatories, Walden Bello of the Philippines and Vandana Shiva of India, have written extensively about globalization, the new global trade agenda, and alternative arrangements. Bello is a prominent advocate of deglobalization, by which he means the removal of all the new rules and regulations of trade, along with the attendant institutions of global governance. The new structures, he argues, constitute an "iron cage" that can only encourage "oligarchic decision-making" and an entrenchment of existing inequalities. The solution, he asserts, lies in "a fluid international system, where there are multiple zones of ambiguity that the less powerful can exploit in order to protect their interests."[53] Elsewhere, Vandana Shiva, a member of the International Forum on Globalization, has argued:

> We want a new millennium based on economic democracy, not economic totalitarianism. The future is possible for humans and other species only if the principles of competition, organized greed, commodification of all life, monocultures and monopolies, and centralized global corporate control of our daily lives enshrined in the WTO are replaced by the principles of protection of people and nature, the obligation of giving and sharing diversity, and the decentralization and self-organization enshrined in our diverse cultures and national constitutions.[54]

And what is occurring "on the ground," in terms of alternatives to neoliberalism? In a recent essay, Naomi Klein has documented political developments in Latin America.[55] She notes that ever since Argentina's financial and political chaos in 2001, elections have brought to power progressive, anti-neoliberal governments in Argentina, Bolivia, Brazil, Chile, Ecuador, Nicaragua, and Venezuela. New policies include nationalization of key sectors of the economy, land reform, and major investments in education, literacy, and health care. The governments of Venezuela, Costa Rica, Argentina, Uruguay, and Bolivia have announced that they will no longer send students to the School of the Americas (now called the Western Hemisphere Institute for Security Cooperation), the police and military training center in Fort Benning, Georgia, that became infamous for graduating future torturers. In Brazil, the farmers of the Landless Workers' Movement (MST) have formed hundreds of cooperatives to reclaim unused land. In Argentina, the movement of "recovered companies" has been led by workers who have resuscitated two hundred bankrupt businesses and turned them into democratically run cooperatives. Venezuelan president Hugo Chávez has made the cooperatives in his own country a top political priority, giving them first refusal on government contracts and offering them economic incentives to trade with one another. Klein also describes the Bolivian Alternative for the Americas (ALBA), "the continent's retort to the Free Trade Area of the Americas, the now-buried corporatist dream of a free-trade zone stretching from Alaska to Tierra del Fuego." In this fair-trade plan, Bolivia provides gas at stable discounted prices; Venezuela offers heavily subsidized oil to poorer countries and shares expertise in developing reserves; and Cuba sends thousands of doctors to deliver free health care all over the continent, while training students from other countries at its medical schools. Last but not least, a "Bank of the South" is planned as a regional alternative to current international financial institutions. It would make loans to member countries and promote economic integration among them. Do these initiatives represent "another world" in practice? It may be too soon to tell, but Klein does suggest that, at the very least, they augur a crisis of credibility for the World Bank, the IMF, and the WTO.

CONCLUSION

In a sense, if contemporary globalization's origins lie in the changes to the world-economy that began in the 1970s and became more visible in the 1980s, then opposition to neoliberal globalization can be regarded as almost continuous. Nevertheless, it has been useful to distinguish two cycles of collective action as well as to establish their connections and their relationship to globalization. Santos correctly notes that the WSF was born in the Global South—at least in the Latin American South—and that it represents "an epistemology of the South." This is an important point which confirms our argument that a connection exists between the activities, institutions, and intellectuals of the contemporary global justice movement and those involved in earlier cycles of mobilizations and protest in the Third World. Such observations, moreover, help to globalize social movement theory.

We have seen how the "movement of movements" has created a dynamic transnational public sphere replete with discussions, debates, research, and collaborative action. The GJM meets in physical space—notably at the World Social Forum and at various other regional forums—but it also has created a virtual community through the Internet. What is more, the global justice movement is—like the women's rights movement—an integral part of global civil society, a democratic sphere beyond the spheres of the state and the market.

The study of the GJM calls into question previous hypotheses and claims regarding the evolution of social movements. In the 1980s and 1990s, some scholars were too quick to argue that the "new social movements" privileged identity, lifestyle, and values (in contradistinction to the "old social movement" issues of class, inequality, and power); that single-issue campaigns were more effective than broad politics; and that lobbying was now the preferred strategy. These hypotheses had been premature even in the 1980s when transnational feminist networks emerged.[56] The Battle of Seattle and events since then have shown that a broad-based politics against economic injustice, inequality, and exploitation could feature as prominently in the twenty-first century as it did in centuries past.

CHAPTER 6

CONCLUSIONS AND PROGNOSTICATION

This book has examined three transnational social movements, their relationship to globalization processes, and similarities and differences among them. Drawing on a number of theoretical frameworks—those of social movements, feminism, the world-system, and the world polity—we have looked at how social movements have responded to political opportunities on a global scale, framed grievances and alternatives, and created new mobilizing structures. In the course of our study, we have drawn attention to the opportunities and resources available for movement-building, the use of violence in social movements and transnational networks, the relationship of war to the global capitalist order, and the salience of masculinities in global processes. This book began by posing a number of questions: What is the connection between globalization and social movements? How have people collectively responded to globalization? Have social movements changed to better confront globalization's economic, political, and cultural manifestations and challenges? And how are contemporary social movements and networks affecting the progression of globalization?

The economic, political, and cultural dimensions of globalization, we have argued, create opportunities and engender grievances that have resulted in at least two forms of collective action responses on a transnational scale: non-violent and progressive, and violent and extremist. We have seen how social movements have utilized technology to their advantage: the Internet, in particular, has become a key mobilizing resource, a framing device, and a means by which collective identities are created and maintained. Although the Internet has not replaced physical sites of recruitment and action, it has enabled the creation of virtual activism and facilitated the emergence of a transnational public sphere. Cyber-networking has helped movement mobilizations to proceed rapidly and effectively, challenging the hegemony of global capital, institutions of global governance, and repressive states. All three movements considered in this book are counter-hegemonic, even though they are starkly different in some ways.

A key difference between the Islamist movement, on the one hand, and the feminist and global justice movements, on the other, lies in the framings as well as the collective action repertoires. Islamists are not preoccupied with neoliberal capitalist globalization; rather, the problem is framed as Western imperialism or cultural invasion or Islam in danger. Global social democracy, or even local democratic practice, is not presented as a solution; rather, "Islam is the solution." In contrast, transnational feminism and global justice have a shared antipathy toward the current model of capitalist globalization and a common commitment to deliberative democratic processes, whether within their own organizations, in inter-group and coalition politics, or in the world-system at large. What is more, while conferences, activist research, lobbying efforts, cyber-activism, protest rallies, and civil disobedience constitute the collective action repertoire of feminist and global justice movements, Islamists deploy militant and violent tactics not only against state repression but also in response to what they perceive as insults to their religion and culture. Moderate Islamists will engage with elections, the media, professional associations, and other societal institutions to extend their influence, but they have not satisfied skeptics who raise questions about Islamist commitment to democratic processes, civil liberties, and inclusive citizenship.

Despite their differences, the three transnational movements originate in the same structural sources: neoliberal inequalities, the global diffusion of world culture, and (to a lesser degree) Internet-based activism. Neoliberal globalization has exacerbated inequalities across and within countries, leading to the emergence of the various types of contenders and challengers that we have examined in this book: jihadists and moderate Islamists, transnational feminists, and global justice activists. The global spread of Western cultural products, discourses, values, and norms has been rejected *tout court* by militant Islamists and selectively by feminists and global justice activists. That is, while transnational feminists and global justice activists embrace the discourses and values of human rights, women's rights, and environmental protection, they reject the dominant values of consumerism, commercialization, and privatization.

If social movements and activism have a place in civil society, then transnational social movements and global civil society are similarly connected. Civil society is a sphere of associational life that provides citizens with an alternative site of engagement and resources outside (and, presumably, beyond the clutches of) the state and the market. Civil society organizations include informal networks, social clubs, voluntary associations, non-state religious organizations, and social movement organizations. Global civil society is made up of those actors that consciously communicate, cooperate, and organize across national boundaries. In this book we have encountered two approaches to civil society, one normative and subjective and the other empirical and objective. Is civil society exclusively a domain of democratic interaction and progressive transformation? Rupert Taylor and his colleagues have argued that it is, but others have noted that non-state actors, including social movements and networks themselves, are diverse and not necessarily emancipatory. According to Guidry, Kennedy, and Zald: "This is not to suggest that social movement theory should abandon the normative impulses that have drawn so many to engagement with movements. Rather, we suggest that it could be driven to engage the resonant and dissonant motifs in the civilizational concerns of movements across the world."[1] In this book, we have done precisely that, by engaging with the dissonant motifs and civilizational concerns of Islamist movements and suggesting that social movements create multiple transnational public spheres that in some cases overlap and in others diverge absolutely.

Paradoxically, then, globalization processes have given rise to both nonviolent democratic movements and violent anti-democratic ones. As Benjamin Barber noted, it was "McWorld" that engendered jihad. But globalization also has been confronted by democratic movements such as feminism and global justice. Scholars have established links between economic globalization and terrorist activity, but also between economic globalization and world culture, on the one hand, and the spread of democratic counter-hegemonic social movements, on the other. If on a conceptual level this duality appears unsatisfying or logically inconsistent, it should be recalled that globalization is a widespread and multi-dimensional process of worldwide restructuring. As such, its entailments and outcomes are not uniform or linear but, rather, contentious and seemingly "messy."

Similarly, social movement theorizing that places a premium on cost-benefit analysis, cool calculations, and strategic thinking in resource mobilizations needs to consider the role of emotions, grievances, moral outrage, and humiliation, as well as joy, commitment, trust, solidarity, and altruism. Social movement activism is neither a matter of individual rational choice nor an example of collective irrationality. It involves people coming together around common grievances, goals, and identities; creating meaning, forging alliances, building coalitions, and maintaining institutions. This work is not an easy task. Constituting, sustaining, or participating in global social movements is a difficult enterprise. Barriers to be overcome are linguistic, monetary, and political—and sometimes cultural. Even beyond the complementarity of agendas and goals, the question of language and communication is central to the ability to meaningfully participate. Within the world of international diplomacy, simultaneous interpretation and rapid translation of documents are common, but the global justice movement, for example, lacks the financial resources for such services. Therefore, much of the work of communicating across language groups other than English, French, and Spanish—for example, at the various meetings of the World Social Forum—is done voluntarily by bilingual or multilingual activists. Multi-lingual websites are certainly helpful—and these are maintained by the World Social Forum as well as by transnational feminist networks such as Women Living Under Muslim Laws and Network Women in Development Europe—but they do not exhaust the languages of large parts of the global community that remain excluded from the deliberative processes of transnational activism.

ON THE MOBILIZING ROLE OF THE INTERNET

Social movement research has shown that recruitment into networks often occurs because of memberships in other networks. This is also known as the friend-of-a-friend phenomenon, or "the strength of weak ties." Activist networks not only ensure that a person is a member of a larger community but also frame issues and offer particular understandings. There is a large body of research on recruitment through networks, but what our analysis has shown is that networks are also created and maintained via the Internet. Sociologist Lauren Langman has argued this point succinctly and well.[2] The Internet provides a variety of "virtual public spheres" where people can find information and "undistorted communication" that highlights adversity and offers frames for understanding that adversity. Virtual public spheres help to foster the embrace of what Manuel Castells has called "project identities." Such identities enable mobilizations that would change that adversity and articulate a vision of what a better policy or law—or indeed, another, better world—might look like. Transnational movements, therefore, can be regarded as *Inter/net/worked movements*. That is, much of their activist work takes place on the Internet; and they are networked with each other both virtually and physically.

If the transnational public sphere is defined as a place where forms of organization and tactics for collective action can be transmitted across the globe, the Internet is a key medium through which this transnational public sphere takes shape. Our study of transnational Islamism, global feminism, and the global justice movement suggests that social movement theorizing needs to consider the mobilizing role of the Internet. The Internet has become a principal site for the formation of political and cultural communities and for the meeting and linking of movement networks. Enabling virtual and transnational public spheres and rapid communication of frames, the Internet allows many movements to connect, thus facilitating the mobilization of "inter-networked" social movements. Solidarities and collective action across borders are of longstanding existence, but the virtual public sphere allows for more rapid dissemination of political expressions and coordination of protest actions—including alerts, appeals, information exchange, petitions, and announcements of public rallies. The Internet enables members of some networks to learn about and join other networks. And it fosters the creation and maintenance of collective identities.

Transnational collective action does not take place exclusively in the virtual sphere, of course. The preceding chapters have shown the importance of recruitment in madrassas, charities, and mosques (Islamist movements), and mobilization processes at international conferences (feminist and global justice movements). Nonetheless, the Internet has become a prime vehicle for the transmission of information about movement strategies, the mobilization of resources, and the exchange of ideas across borders, boundaries, and barriers. For example, the solidarity work of WLUML is maintained through the activities of "networkers." Much of its mobilizing work is done via the Internet, in the form of e-campaigns for women's human rights. The network WIDE does hold an annual conference, and members are found at the World Social Forum and regional forums, but a major part of its work is conducted over the Internet, in the form of newsletters regularly disseminated to the organization's membership list, and an extensive website with postings of research results, advocacy efforts, reports, news, and alerts. The Internet has enabled transnational feminist networks to quickly come to the assistance of their sisters in need, especially those in repressive environments. In 2007 and 2008, for example, transnational feminist networks such as WLUML, DAWN, the Women's Learning Partnership, and Equality Now—along with individual Iranian feminist expatriates—disseminated information, transmitted petitions, and mobilized media interest around the One Million Signatures Campaign inside Iran (for law reform and women's rights), cases of imminent stonings of women charged with adultery, and the closure of a prominent Iranian women's magazine, *Zanan*. These examples make clear that the communications revolution associated with globalization enables actors to participate in collective action, in transnational advocacy networks, and in global social movements via cyberspace while also helping to build a kind of cyber-democracy. The local and the global are now linked in virtual public spheres, allowing activists to communicate, coordinate, exchange information, learn from each other, and build their collective identities and action repertoires across borders and indeed continents. In an era of globalization, mobilization processes have not replaced the traditional sites of family, neighborhood, religious groups, and political networks, but they now extend to the virtual public sphere. As such, the Internet not only augments mobilization processes but sometimes also allows activists to circumvent obstacles and barriers created by repressive states. And in democratic polities where movement activity might be ignored by commercialized media, the Internet can provide alternative sources of information about movement strategies and achievements.

THREE PROPOSITIONS

Chapter 1 summarized this book's main arguments, assumptions, and concepts in nine propositions, largely informed by the effects of globalization on social movements. Here I offer an additional three propositions to serve as food for thought and suggestions for future research on social movements, whether nationally based or transnational. These points pertain to the relationship between states and social movements in the era of globalization; violence and social movements; and gender and social movements.

1. **States and social movements in a globalizing era.** Social movements or networks of contenders take on a transnational form when a) global opportunities for legitimation or growth present themselves (that is, world culture or world society integration), or b) when collective action within domestic/national boundaries is foreclosed or repressed. We will continue to see social movements emerging throughout the world, and their prospects and scope will depend on the combination of political opportunities, both domestic and global, as well as the strength of their mobilizing and framing efforts. Movements are sometimes constrained from transnational activism and sometimes make strategic choices to remain domestically oriented. Globalization of course presents new opportunities for social movements to expand transnationally, but doing so will depend on the strategic choice of the movement involved and the domestic structure of political opportunity.

2. **Violence and social movements.** Social movements or networks of contenders assume violent methods to achieve their goals when a) state repression forecloses open forms of collective action or protest, b) movements or networks interpret repression as weakness or betrayal or an opportunity to gain adherents to the cause, or c) an extant cultural frame can be drawn upon to justify such actions. Violence as a tactic of contentious politics has been largely associated with revolutions or armed rebellions and less so with social movements, although some radical wings of social movements have been known to turn to violent means. State repression can leave a movement with little choice but to take up arms, and in some cultural contexts violence can be justified in religious terms. However, movements have been known to make a strategic choice not to engage in violence, even when states have taken repressive measures against them. Women's movements are invariably non-violent.

3. **Feminism, masculinities, and social movements.** The more masculine the composition and the more violent the discourse, the less likely it is that women will be involved as participants or leaders. Although some women will continue to identify with or support a masculinized movement, and the group may use some women in an instrumental fashion, such movements are unlikely to attract a critical

mass of women or to incorporate them into leadership roles. With transnational networks in particular, which require a high degree of mobility, membership in movements and networks that deploy violence as the chief means of contention will continue to be overwhelmingly male.

IS ANOTHER WORLD POSSIBLE?

All three transnational movements examined in this book express dissatisfaction with the state of the contemporary world and existing power relations. Members of all three believe that another world is possible, even though the Islamist vision may differ markedly from that of feminists and global justice activists. What, indeed, are the prospects for global change, and what are the prospects for our social movements?

In examining the rise of Islamist movements, we have emphasized macro processes such as authoritarianism, economic crisis, and neoliberalism; normative disruptions caused by structural strains; the conservative tendencies of the lower middle class and the petty bourgeoisie; and the militarist implications of hegemonic masculinities. What of the future? Since at least the mid-1990s a debate has ensued among scholars concerning the future of political Islam, especially the future of global jihadism. Some are arguing that militant Islam has exhausted its possibilities and is on the decline. Due to their incompetence and repression, the regimes in Afghanistan, the Islamic Republic of Iran, and Sudan do not constitute a model of governance or state-society relations. The extreme violence of jihadist groups has repelled Muslims across the globe, and many militant groups have been defeated by harsh state repression or the "global war on terror." (The U.S.–U.K. invasion of Iraq has had the opposite effect of stimulating Islamist revival and reaction in that country.) At the same time, religious politics appear strong and are likely to dominate elections, lawmaking, and civil society activism for the foreseeable future. All Muslim countries have populations of liberal, left-wing, or secular citizens, and all have feminist groups. However, many parts of the Muslim world still exhibit the master frames of nationalism and Islam, with the result that we are likely to see the persistence of politics conducted in a religious idiom. Depending on local circumstances, the religious frame will be stronger or weaker in different Muslim-majority countries (including those in the Middle East and North Africa), and it remains to be seen if, or when, Islamism will take the form of movements and political parties that reconcile faith and heritage with "world society" links to global institutions and ideals. (This has already occurred in Turkey, with the AKP.) In the meantime, transnational feminist networks and the global justice movement would do well to support and encourage democratic and progressive forces within Muslim-majority countries while continuing to oppose hegemonic politics, war, and empire.

The women's movement has been among the most successful social movements of the modern era, and feminists around the world continue to associate modernity with women's equality and rights. This is especially the case with feminist activism in countries of the Middle East and North Africa. For example, in her discussion of competing gender frames in contentious Algeria in the 1990s, Doria Cherifati-Merabtine distinguished the "Islamic female ideal" from the "modernist model."[3] Historically, women's movements have been allied with nationalist movements and with liberalism, socialism, and social democracy, and they continue to engage in coalitions with other social forces, movements, and organizations. Yet such groups are increasingly inclined to maintain their autonomy and engage in coalitions only when women's strategic interests are served rather than sidelined. This is evidence of the continuing maturity of women's social movements and especially of feminist ones, which have clear goals about gender hierarchy, democratic transformations, and women's rights. For these reasons feminist groups express strong criticism of Islamist movements and other forms of religio-politics or fundamentalism. There is more of a natural affinity with the global justice movement, even though some tensions have been discerned.

With transnational feminism, the global justice movement shares a critique of neoliberalism, hegemonic governance, war, and all forms of oppression. Like global feminism, which is comprised of many transnational feminist groups with their own frames and strategies, the GJM is a broad global "movement of movements" that has no centralized leadership. (In this respect it is also similar to transnational Islamism.) Some scholar-activists have argued that for the global justice movement to more effectively challenge the hegemony of neoliberal capitalism, it needs more focus, better coordination, stronger leadership, and a more coherent strategy for action and change. As we have seen, however, others prefer that the global justice movement, and the World Social Forum itself, be as inclusive as possible and remain primarily a site for dialogue and diversity, including many different forms of action. It remains to be seen whether the global justice movement can maintain the momentum that it has had over the past few years of the new millennium. Will it be able to present itself as an alternative form of political organizing and—along with progressive governments in Latin America and elsewhere—force changes in the institutions of global governance? Or will the GJM become an alternative cultural site, devoid of political power and unable to exert authority and influence over the workings of the global economy, its institutions, and its agents?

And what of the prospects of globalization itself? If globalization is a "project" with distinct institutions and agents (the "globalizers"), then a strong global justice movement could conceivably force some changes. If, however, globalization is part of a secular historic trend with deep structural roots ("the latest stage of capitalism"), it might need more time to work its way through its own dynamics and contradictions, and it might even exhaust itself as a result of a series of accumulation or legitimation crises. In a reflection of the paradoxes of historical capitalism, the current form of globalization could have a positive impact on some parts of the world, such as the Middle East and North Africa. Already we see that the most globalized parts of the region, notably the Gulf sheikhdoms (though not yet Saudi Arabia), are turning their backs on previously exclusionary politics and responding to "world values." In the United Arab Emirates, for example, which has been enjoying huge investments in international banks, properties, and retail, the first parliamentary elections in 2007 brought about a 23 percent share of women, and there have been public dialogues about the rights of migrant workers and other previously excluded groups. As the Middle East becomes more integrated into world society, could we see a concerted movement toward less contentious politics?

There are two possible directions that globalization in the Middle East could take. In one, international links would lead to political and cultural liberalization, including the growth of civil society and campaigns for human rights and expanded concepts of citizenship. This route could end the kind of vulnerability that allows the hegemonic power to seek to assert control (as with the invasion and occupation of Iraq by the United States); and it could end the anger, frustration, and humiliation that have driven Islamist movements. Conversely, transnational links and growing economic influence could provide additional resources to Islamic institutions and networks, including militant ones, with the effect of expanding their global reach. In this scenario, competition increases and divergences are enhanced. In the more positive scenario, however, "world values" are expanded in a way that suggests cultural and political convergence, and the hegemonic power is itself marginalized. We can only wait and hope—but act, too.

NOTES

CHAPTER 1: INTRODUCTION AND OVERVIEW

1. For example, Frobel et al. 1980; Chase-Dunn 1989.

2. For example, McAdam, McCarthy, and Zald 1996; Melucci 1996.

3. Cox 1992; Moghadam 1993; Hopkins and Wallerstein 1996; Boswell and Chase-Dunn 2000.

4. Steger 2002; Sklair 2001, 2002. See Fukuyama 1992 for a celebration of what he sees as the triumph of liberal democracy and capitalism at the end of the Cold War.

5. Meyer, Boli, Thomas, and Ramirez 1997; Boli and Thomas 1997; Smith, Chatfield, and Pagnucco 1997; Keck and Sikkink 1998; Boli 2005.

6. On gender and fundamentalism see Kandiyoti 1991 and Moghadam 1994. On Islamist movements, see Zubaida 1993. See also Beckford 1986 for comparative perspectives, and Marty and Appleby's four volumes on comparative fundamentalisms (1991, 1992, 1993, 1994).

7. Smith et al. 1997; Keck and Sikkink 1998.

8. Guidry, Kennedy, and Zald 2000; Smith and Johnston 2002; Podobnik and Reifer 2004; Appelbaum and Robinson 2005; Moghadam 2005; Chase-Dunn and Babones 2006; della Porta 2007.

9. Keck and Sikkink 1998: 3.

10. Marchand and Runyan 2000; Meyer and Prugl 1999; Moghadam 2005; Stienstra 2000.

11. Tarrow 1994: 48, cited in Keck and Sikkink 1998: 37.

12. Heckscher 2002.

13. Polanyi 2001. Karl Polanyi's highly influential text was originally published in 1944. The 2001 edition includes contributions by economist Joseph Stiglitz and political sociologist Fred Block.

14. Keck and Sikkink 1998: 38.

15. Moaddel 2005: 9.

16. Salafiyists are literalists who also believe that Muslims should be ruled by an Islamic state similar to that established by the prophet Mohammad and his successors (the *salaf*). They formed partly in opposition to folkloric versions of Islam (maraboutism) practiced by rural people and urban poor.

17. Voll 1991, cited in Marty and Appleby 1991.

18. Esposito 2002: 45–46.

19. Boxer and Quataert 1978. The socialist movement organized predominantly working-class women, such as textile workers, for revolutionary causes, while the feminist organizations were largely middle-class and reformist.

20. Jayawardena 1986.

21. See Berkovitch 1999; Meyer 1999; Rupp 1998; Stienstra 1994.

22. See Chase-Dunn 1998.

23. These arguments are associated with, respectively, Harvey 2003, Robinson 2004, Pieterse 2004.

24. Wallerstein 2000, 2003.

25. McAdam, McCarthy, and Zald 1996.

26. Snow 2004.

27. Gerlach 1999: 95.

28. See Goodwin, Jasper, and Polleta 2001; Flam and King 2005.

29. Cited in Barkawi 2006: 130. The quote is from a videotaped statement released on October 7, 2001. The mention of "eighty years" is a reference to the downfall and breakup of the Ottoman Empire and its caliphate.

30. In her feminist analysis of globalization, Spike Peterson (2003) has identified three gendered economic spheres: that of the production of goods and the provision of services; that of social, biological, and labor reproduction (sometimes known as the care economy); and the sphere of non-material, speculative, and financial transactions (the virtual economy).

31. The term is from Guidry, Kennedy, and Zald 2000: 17, but I am not suggesting that they would agree with my recommendation.

32. Reid and Chen 2007.

33. On critical globalization studies, see Appelbaum and Robinson 2005.

CHAPTER 2:
GLOBALIZATION AND COLLECTIVE ACTION

1. Barnet and Muller 1974. See Roberts and Hite 2007 for an elaboration of this evolution.

2. Klein 2007.

3. Soviet support was especially important to the South African and Palestinian liberation movements.

4. See "Declaration on the Establishment of a New International Economic Order," reprinted in Broad 2002: 99–102.

5. Loans also were taken out by dictators, which helped to entrench their rule and benefited the lending institutions to the detriment of citizens. Such loans later came to be called "odious" by advocates of debt cancellation. See chapter 5.

6. Payer 1975.

7. For more details, see Marglin and Schor 1990.

8. Rupert and Solomon 2006: 42.

9. Harvey 2003, 2004; Robinson 2004.

10. Wallerstein 1991; Chase-Dunn 1998.

11. Yaghmaian 2001.

12. Sklair 2001, 2002; Steger 2002.

13. Bello 2000; Khor 2000; Korten 1995; Mander 1996.

14. As early as 1978, Professor James Tobin, winner of the 1981 Nobel Prize for Economics, proposed a tax on international currency transactions (for example, foreign exchange speculation) to reduce the volatility and instability of financial markets. (See his paper "A Proposal for International Monetary Reform," *Eastern Economic Journal* 4, nos. 3–4 [July/October 1978]: 153–59.) In 1994 he reiterated his proposal, suggesting that the proceeds of that tax be placed at the disposition of international organizations for development purposes. The idea for such a tax was endorsed by many progressive NGOs, including transnational feminist networks, and became a principal demand of ATTAC, which went on to become a key group within the GJM. The Tobin tax was discussed by NGOs at the 1995 UN Social Summit in Copenhagen but was turned down by most governments. James Tobin died in March 2002. For a movement perspective on the Tobin tax, see Round 2002.

15. See the summary of Maddison's research in UNDP 1999. See also Atkinson 2001; Taylor 2000.

16. Milanovic 2005.

17. UNDP 1999; Oxfam 2002. See essays by Stiglitz and by Sachs, in Roberts and Hite 2007.

18. Mathews 1997: 50; Strange 1996: 4; Beck 2004: 144.

19. Castells 1997, cited in Zivkovic and Hogan 2007: 186.

20. Sklair 1991, 2001; Chase-Dunn 1998. Sklair (2001: 1) argues that "the transnational capitalist class has transformed capitalism into a globalizing project," while Robinson and Harris (2000: 20) state that "the transnationalization of the capital circuit implies as well the transnationalization of the agents of capital."

21. Hirst and Thompson 1996; Berger and Dore 1996.

22. Tarrow 2001.

23. Barkawi 2006: 10.

24. Santos 2006. See also chapter 5 in this book.

25. Scholte 2000: 46; Pieterse 1998. See also Held 2000.

26. Barber 2001.

27. Barber 2001: 232.

28. Barber 2001: i.

29. My use of the term "Empire" differs from that of Hardt and Negri (2000), who theorized away the militarized state and coercive international relations, and disputed the hegemonic role of the United States.

30. On the importance of the Afghanistan episode, see Cooley 1999; Rashid 2000; and Moghadam 2003: chapter 7.

31. On this latter point, see Elizabeth Drew, "The War in Washington," *New York Review of Books* (May 10, 2007): 53–55.

32. David Harvey has correctly termed the American enterprise in Iraq a return to primitive accumulation.

33. Connell 1998.

34. For example, in Muslim cultures, female modesty is valued much more than sexual availability. And rather than intense interest in sexual conquest, hegemonic masculinity in, for example, a typical Middle Eastern context might consist in the capacity to protect family or personal honor by controlling the comportment of the women in the family, or in the community, or in the nation.

35. Langman and Morris 2004.

36. Runyan 2000: 362.

37. Barber 2001; Kaldor 2003; Chua 2003.

38. Eckstein and Wickham-Crowley 2003. See also Johnston and Almeida 2006.

39. Hadden and Tarrow 2007: 214; Tarrow 2005: 11.

40. See Moghadam 2005; see also Red and Chen 2007.

41. Smith and Wiest 2005; Lizardo 2006; Wiest 2007.

42. Alger, in Smith et al. 1997: 262, table 15.1.

43. See Guidry, Kennedy, and Zald 2000: 3.

44. Pianta and Marchetti 2007: 30–31.

45. Kaldor 2003: 44–45; 46.

46. Anheier, Glasius, and Kaldor 2001: 21.

47. Bauer and Hélie 2006.

48. Taylor 2004: 4.

CHAPTER 3: ISLAMIST MOVEMENTS

1. Gerges 2005; Wiktorowicz 2004: 15; Hafez 2003.

2. See, for example, Rahman 1982. Fazlur Rahman was a critic of political and theological dogmatism whose career included a senior civil service post in Pakistan and a professorship at the University of Chicago. See also Charles Kurzman's liberal Islam project: http://www.unc.edu/~kurzman/LiberalIslamLinks.htm.

3. While they attracted many supporters in Iran and the diaspora, the religious intellectuals—Abdolkarim Soroush; Mohsen Saidzadeh; Mohsen Kadivar; Hasan Yousefi Eshkevari; Mohammad Mojtahed Shabestari—have been harassed or forced into exile by the authorities. For more information on these proponents of a liberal Islam, see Kurzman's online sources; see also Mir-Hosseini and Tapper (2006).

4. See Fourest 2004.

5. Wiktorowicz 2004: 2; Hafez 2003: 5.

6. Sadik Jalal Al-Azm, "What Is Islamism?" Unpublished paper, given to me by the author, Damascus, December 17, 2007.

7. Amin 2007: 2. That Islamist movements are right-wing as well as patriarchal has long been argued by transnational feminists such as Marieme Hélie-Lucas, a founder of Women Living Under Muslim Laws. See chapter 4 for details.

8. Of course, Islam did not spread by the sword alone. Trade, empire, and settlement by Muslims helped the community to grow, while the decency of their Muslim neighbors encouraged others to convert.

9. Barnett Rubin mentions the importance of Kuwaiti as well as Saudi money for the Afghan mujahideen as well as other militant Islamist groups. See Rubin 1997, where he describes the "arms pipeline."

10. See Esposito 1989.

11. Cooley 1999: 1.

12. Ibrahim 1980.

13. At least one scholar, however, sees similarities between contemporary Islamists and the extreme left in Europe in the 1970s. Sadik Al-Azm's views on the matter will be presented later in this chapter.

14. See, inter alia, Mernissi 1987; Kandiyoti 1991; Moghadam 1994.

15. These propositions were earlier presented in the first (1993) edition of my book *Modernizing Women: Gender and Social Change in the Middle East*. They are also included in that book's second edition. The propositions remain valid and I present them here with minor editing. See Moghadam 2003: chapter 5 for bibliographic details.

16. The origin of the name "al-Qaeda" is somewhat unclear; it may refer to a "base" used by bin Laden and his associates in Afghanistan. See Halliday 2005: 196.

17. Gerges 2005. See also Johnson 2001.

18. Moghadam 1994.

19. Wiktorowicz, p. 16.

20. Cesari 2004.

21. Olesen 2007: 42.

22. Entelis 2005.

23. Wiktorowicz 2004: 20.

24. Hafez 2004; Hafez 2003.

25. Hafez and Wiktorowicz 2004: 62.

26. Moghadam 2001.

27. Hafez 2004: 48–49.

28. Hafez 2004: 50.

29. Hafez 2004: 52.

30. See Goodwin 2007.

31. Goodwin 2001.

32. Gulalp 2001: 434.

33. Gulalp 2001.
34. Brown, Hamzawy, and Ottaway 2006: 7.
35. See, for example, Tariq Ramadan, in *The Fundamentalisms Project*, volume 3.
36. Abdo 2000.
37. Brown, Hamzawy, and Ottaway 2006.
38. David Wroe, "Divisions in the Muslim Brotherhood," http://www.theage.com.au/news/world/divisions-in-muslim-brotherhood/2007/11/16/1194766965617.html (November 17). (Accessed December 12, 2007.)
39. El-Ghobashy 2005: 391.
40. Fuller 2002: 52–53.
41. Schwedler 2006; Langohr 2001.
42. An example is the Red Mosque affair in Islamabad, Pakistan, in July 2007, when thousands of militants associated with the mosque and its affiliated schools barricaded themselves with arms until military units eventually attacked.
43. Clark 2004; Harik 2004.
44. Wiktorowicz 2004.
45. Al-Mahajiroun was disbanded in 2004 and its leader Omar Bakri Mohammad has not been allowed back into the United Kingdom since August 2005. It tenet was "the use of military coups to establish Islamic states wherever there are Muslims, including Britain" (Wiktorowicz 2005: 7). Considered by many U.K. Muslims as a "lunatic fringe," it managed to elicit considerable media attention.
46. Ian Black, "Al-Qaida Chief Launched 'Any Questions' Sessions on Web," *The Guardian* (December 20, 2007): 22.
47. Anna Johnson, "Al-Qaida Member Says Bush Should Be Greeted in Mideast with Bombs," Associated Press (January 7, 2008).
48. Steger 2003: 5, 2.
49. Khosrokhavar 2005.
50. Al-Azm 2004. Sadik Jalal Al-Azm, retired professor of modern European philosophy at the University of Damascus, is one of the most prominent critical intellectuals in the Arab world.
51. Al-Azm 2004: 19.
52. Ibid.: 19–20.
53. Ibid.: 20–21.
54. Pasha and Samatar 1997: 200.
55. Huntington 1996.

CHAPTER 4: FEMINISM ON A WORLD SCALE

1. See, for example, Chafetz and Dworkin 1986; Dahlerup 1987; Margolis 1993; Basu 1995.
2. Stienstra 1994, 2000; Naples and Desai 2002; Moghadam 2005.
3. Sperling, Ferree, and Risman 2001: 1157.
4. Hawkesworth 2006: 27.

5. Moghadam 2005.

6. The Fourth World Conference on Women gathered to discuss, finalize, and adopt the draft Beijing Platform for Action, which identified twelve "critical areas of concern," including education, health, employment, poverty, the girl-child, and decision-making.

7. The Palestinian question also divided participants, especially at the Copenhagen NGO Forum. See Fraser 1987.

8. Women-in-development (WID) began in the early 1970s and sought to bring attention to the problems facing women in the development process, including their marginalization from productive activities. Women-and-development (WAD) emerged as a more critical turn, and researchers raised questions about the nature of the development process that women were to be integrated into. (See Beneria and Sen 1981; Elson and Pearson 1981.) The gender-and-development (GAD) approach grounded itself more explicitly in feminist theorizing. (See Young 1992.)

9. Standing 1989, 1999.

10. Moghadam 1993; Rueschemeyer 1998.

11. Beneria and Feldman 1992; Chant 1995.

12. For an elaboration of various types of fundamentalism, their gender dynamics, and their impacts on women's legal status and social positions, see contributions in Kandiyoti 1991 and Moghadam 1994, 1995.

13. Moghadam 2003, chapter 7.

14. WIDE 1998; Wichterich 1999.

15. For details on the activities of transnational feminist networks such as DAWN, WIDE, and WEDO, see Moghadam 2005: chapter 5.

16. French-speaking North African feminists were able to connect relatively easily with the Québec-based World March of Women.

17. ICFTU, "3,000 Trade Unionists March in Protest at Poverty and Violence against Women in Durban on April 5." www.icftu.org. (Accessed April 15, 2002.) The ICFTU is now known as the International Trade Union Confederation, or ITUC, a nod to post–Cold War realities.

18. Moghadam 2005: 75–76.

19. Dufour and Giraud 2007: 310.

20. Ibid.: 318–19.

21. Kazi 1997: 141.

22. See http://www.learningpartnership.org.

23. Hélie-Lucas 1993: 225.

24. This cautionary message was stated at a conference I organized on comparative fundamentalisms and women, which took place at UNU/WIDER in Helsinki, Finland, in October 1990. See Moghadam 1994.

25. Boix 2001: 6.

26. Personal communication from Marieme Hélie-Lucas, July 3, 2003. Charlotte Bunch, founder-director of the Center for Women's Global Leadership at Rutgers

University, was instrumental not only in raising funds for women's groups and their meetings but also in conceptualizing women's rights in the private sphere as human rights. For details on Algerian women's organizations, see Moghadam 2003, chapters 3 and 8. Details about Khalida Messaoudi, who became a cabinet minister in summer 2002, are available on the Algerian government website; see also Messaoudi and Schemla 1995.

27. Shaheed 1994: 7–8.

28. Boix 2001: 7.

29. http://wluml.org/english/pubsfulltxt.shtml?cmd[87]=i-87-549649. (Accessed January 16, 2008.)

30. http://wluml.org/english/links.shtml. (Accessed January 16, 2008.)

31. Enloe 2007: 14.

32. See, for example, Enloe 1990, 2007; Reardon 1993; Tickner 1992; Accad 2007; Flamhaft 2007; Moghadam 2007.

33. Pietila and Vickers 1994.

34. Lucille Mathurin Mair was secretary-general of the United Nations' second conference on women, which convened in Copenhagen in 1980. The passage is cited in Bunch and Carillo 1992: 71.

35. See http://www.un.org/docs/scres.

36. Jang Roko Abhiyan, "Rally on the 25th [of September, 2001]," circulated via Internet by socglob@topica.com.

37. Eleanor Smeal (president of the Feminist Majority), "Special Message from the Feminist Majority on the Taliban, Osama bin Laden, and Afghan Women." September 18, 2001. http://feministmajority.org.

38. From http://www.IWTC.org.

39. Starhawk 2003: 17.

40. Communicated to the author via e-mail in 2003.

41. The quotes appear on pages 62, 65, and 66, respectively, of the spring 2003 issue of Ms. magazine.

42. This occurred on October 24, 2007, and was widely reported. Rice had been on Capitol Hill to testify before the House Foreign Relations Committee.

43. Milazzo 2005: 103. See also Brim 2003: 10–12.

44. See http://www.nobelwomensinitative.org. The present author was an invited participant. The six founders are Shirin Ebadi of Iran, Jody Williams of the United States, Betty Williams and Mairead Corrigan of Northern Ireland, Wangari Matthai of Kenya, and Rigoberta Menchu of Guatemala. The first international conference took place in Galway, Ireland, in May 2007, and was attended by about seventy-five women from across the globe.

45. Eisenstein 2004.

46. Enloe 2007.

47. Vargas 2005: 109–10.

48. Bach 2004.

49. Alexander and Mbali 2004.

50. WLUML 2005.

51. Tariq Ramadan is considered by many observers to be an important intellectual and a representative of a liberal or moderate Islam. But others view him with skepticism. For a critique of Tariq Ramadan's Arabic-language statements, see Fourest 2004. Caroline Fourest—who also has authored a scathing critique of the French far-right nationalist leader Le Pen—notes that in one of Ramadan's cassettes he deliberately conflates "so-called secular Muslims" with "Muslims lacking Islam" (p.149). He also calls veiling a Muslim obligation and encourages young women to defend their right to veil, in part to protect themselves against the male gaze (see Fourest, p. 212, quoting another cassette). At the first International Congress of Islamic Feminism, held in Barcelona in late October 2005 and organized by the Junta Islamica Catalan and the UNESCO office in Barcelona, Zainah Anwar of the Malaysian group Sisters in Islam told me that Tariq Ramadan had defended *hijab* at a meeting in Kuala Lumpur, leading to a spirited debate with the Islamic feminists who are themselves not veiled.

52. Vargas 2005: 109.

CHAPTER 5: THE GLOBAL JUSTICE MOVEMENT

1. See, for example, della Porta 2007.

2. Taylor 1993, 2000.

3. Njehu 2004: 103.

4. Bello 2000: 55.

5. Subcomandante Marcos 2004.

6. Njehu 2004.

7. The G-7 became the G-8 with the inclusion of Russia.

8. George 2004: 194. Susan George, a veteran international activist, goes on to say that Jubilee 2000 dissolved itself in the year 2000, while other groups within the GJM continue to campaign for the abolition of all Third World debt.

9. George 2004: 196.

10. For details, see Moghadam 2005, chapter 3.

11. See, for example, Langman, Morris, and Zalewski 2002.

12. On the Tobin tax, see chapter 2.

13. Bello 2004: 55. Bello adds that "the war on terror" resulted in a return of the U.S. military bases.

14. Bello 2004: 64.

15. Pianta and Marchetti 2007: 40–41.

16. Podobnik 2005.

17. Moghadam 2005: 31–32; Pianta and Marchetti 2007: 40–41.

18. Various news reports covered the protest events of the early 2000s—for example, Tom Hundley, "Anti-Globalization Groups Gear Up," *Chicago Tribune* (July

15, 2001); Ben White, "An Elite Cast Debates Poverty," *Washington Post* (February 3, 2002); and Leslie Crawford, "Huge Protest March Passes Off Peacefully," *Financial Times* (March 18, 2002).

19. Pianta and Marchetti 2007: 39.

20. Vargas 2005.

21. Reese, Gutierrez, and Chase-Dunn 2007: 4.

22. della Porta 2007: 44.

23. For example, in West Lafayette, Indiana, where this book's author is based, the global justice movement is present in the form of an anti-sweatshop student group at Purdue University called POLE (Purdue Organization for Labor Equality), and a community group called the Greater Lafayette Progressive Alliance. Members of both attended the United States Social Forum that took place in Atlanta, Georgia, in July 2007.

24. See http://www.attac.org, and George 2004: xi.

25. Ancelovici 2002.

26. Reese et al. 2007: 6.

27. Mertes 2004: 242.

28. Reese et al. 2007: 6.

29. See also Smith et al. 2008.

30. Reese et al. 2007 surveyed 640 participants (out of 155,000 registered participants from 135 countries) at the 2005 WSF in Porto Alegre, and found the following demographic breakdown: South Americans represented 68 percent of those surveyed (with Brazilians making up 58 percent of the total number); Western Europeans 13 percent; North Americans 9 percent; Asians 8 percent; and Africans 2 percent. Their sample included no participants from the Middle East or North Africa.

31. Santos 2006: 95.

32. Reese et al. 2007.

33. Santos 2006: 104. See also http://www.forumsocialmundial.org.br.

34. Santos 2006: 188–95 (appendix 1).

35. Borland 2006.

36. IGTN 2002.

37. Santos 2006: 53–54.

38. Santos 2006: 60.

39. See *Declaration of the 2003 World Social Forum: Perspective of Women of the World March of Women*, at http://www.marchemondiale.org and http://www.ffq.qc.ca/marche2000.

40. Santos 2006: 35.

41. http://www.forumsocialmundial.org.br/main.php?id_menu=4&cd_language=2.

42. Santos 2006: 92–93.

43. Those in favor of more deliberate action issued the Manifesto of Porto Alegre, which is discussed below.

44. Santos 2006: 111–26.

45. Reese et al. 2007. Many European activists feel that a strong EU is needed as a counterweight to U.S. hegemony, but others in the GJM are opposed and prefer a return to local democracy.

46. Pianta and Marchetti 2007: 48.

47. Cited in George 2004: 98.

48. See contributions in Podobnik and Reifer 2004; see also George 2004.

49. Susan George was among the participants of a landmark conference, organized by left-wing sociology professors and held at the University of California, Santa Barbara, in May 2003, that sought to define and advance "critical globalization studies." Her presentation focused on the responsibility of scholar-activists.

50. George 2004.

51. Santos 2006: 205–7 (appendix 3). The Bamako Appeal of 2006 makes a similar set of proposals. See http://mrzine.monthlyreview.org/bamako.html.

52. See Broad 2002: 42–46. The statement was issued and signed, inter alia, by Maude Barlow (Council of Canadians), Walden Bellow (Focus on the Global South), Lori Wallach (Public Citizen), Vandana Shiva, and John Cavanaugh.

53. Bello 2000: 90.

54. Shiva 2000: 123–24.

55. Klein 2007.

56. Moghadam 2005.

CHAPTER 6:
CONCLUSIONS AND PROGNOSTICATION

1. Guidry, Kennedy, and Zald 2000: 24.

2. Langman 2005.

3. Cherifati-Merabtine 1995: 42.

REFERENCES

Abdo, Geneive. 2000. *No God but God: Egypt and the Triumph of Islam*. Oxford: Oxford University Press.

Accad, Evelyne. 2007. "Gender and Violence in Lebanese War Novels." Pp. 293–310 in *From Patriarchy to Empowerment: Women's Participation, Movements, and Rights in the Middle East, North Africa, and South Asia*, edited by V. M. Moghadam. Syracuse, NY: Syracuse University Press.

Al-Azm, Sadik. 2004. "Islam, Terrorism and the West Today." Essay written for the Praemium Esarmianum Foundation on the occasion of the award of the Erasmus Prize, Amsterdam (November). Naarden: Foundation Horizon.

Alexander, Amanda, and Mandisa Mbali. 2004. "Have the Slaves Left the Master's House?" A report on the Africa Social Forum. *Alternatives . . . for a Different World* (December 21). http://www.alternatives.ca/article1625.html. (Last accessed January 16, 2008.)

Alexander, Christopher. 2000. "Opportunities, Organizations, and Ideas: Islamists and Workers in Tunisia and Algeria." *International Journal of Middle East Studies* 32 (2000): 465–90.

Amin, Samir. 2007. "Political Islam in the Service of Imperialism." *Monthly Review* (December): 1–18.

Ancelovici, Marcos. 2002. "Organizing against Globalization: The Case of ATTAC in France." *Politics & Society* 30, no. 3 (September): 427–63.

Anderson, Sarah, ed. 2000. *Views from the South: The Effects of Globalization and the WTO on Third World Countries*. Chicago: Food First Books.

Anheier, Helmut, Marlies Glasius, and Mary Kaldor, eds. 2001. *The Global Civil Society Yearbook*. Oxford: Oxford University Press.

Applebaum, Richard, and William I. Robinson, eds. 2005. *Critical Globalization Studies*. New York: Routledge.

Atkinson, Anthony. 2001. "Is Rising Inequality Inevitable? A Critique of the Transatlantic Consensus." WIDER Annual Lectures 3. Helsinki: UNU/WIDER (November).

Bach, Amandine. 2004. "The Third European Social Forum, London, 14–17 October 2004." http://62.149.193.10/wide/download/The%203rd%20ESF.pdf?id=250. (Last accessed January 12, 2008.)

Barber, Benjamin. 2001. *Jihad vs. McWorld*. New York: Times Books.

Barkawi, Tarak. 2006. *Globalization and War*. Lanham, MD: Rowman & Littlefield.

Barnet, Richard J., and Ronald Muller. 1974. *Global Reach: The Power of Multinational Corporations*. New York: Simon & Shuster.

Basu, Amrita, ed. 1995. *The Challenge of Local Feminisms: Women's Movements in Global Perspective*. Boulder: Westview Press.

Bauer, Jan, and Anissa Hélie. 2006. *Documenting Women's Human Rights Violations by Non-State Actors: Activist Strategies from Muslim Communities*. Québec: International Centre for Human Rights and Democratic Development and WLUML.

Beck, Ulrich. 2004. "The Cosmopolitan Turn." Pp. 143–66 in *The Future of Social Theory*, edited by Nicholas Gane. London: Continuum.

Beckford, James, ed. 1986. *New Religious Movements and Rapid Social Change*. Thousand Oaks, CA, and Paris: Sage and UNESCO.

Bello, Walden. 2004. "The Global South." Pp. 49–69 in *A Movement of Movements: Is Another World Really Possible?* edited by Tom Mertes. London: Verso.

———. 2000. "Building an Iron Cage." Pp. 54–90 in *Views from the South: The Effects of Globalization and the WTO on Third World Countries*, edited by Sarah Anderson. Chicago: Food First and the International Forum on Globalization.

Beneria, Lourdes, and Gita Sen. 1981. "Accumulation, Reproduction and Women's Role in Development: Boserup Revisited." *Signs* 8, no. 2 (Winter).

Beneria, Lourdes, and Shelley Feldman, eds. 1992. *Unequal Burden: Economic Crises, Persistent Poverty, and Women's Work*. Boulder: Westview Press.

Berger, Suzanne, and Ronald Dore, eds. 1996. *National Diversity and Global Capitalism*. Ithaca, NY: Cornell University Press.

Berkovitch, Nitza. 1999. *From Motherhood to Citizenship: Women's Rights and International Organizations*. Baltimore: Johns Hopkins University Press.

Boix, Monserrat. 2001. "Women's Networks: Islamists' Violence and Terror." *WLUML Newsheet* 13, no. 4 (November–December).

Boli, John. 2005. "Contemporary Developments in World Culture." *International Journal of Contemporary Sociology* 46 (5–6): 383–404.

Boli, John, and George M. Thomas. 1997. "World Culture in the World Polity." *American Sociological Review* 62, no. 2 (April): 171–90.

Borland, Elizabeth. 2006. "The Mature Resistance of Argentina's Madres de Plaza de Mayo." Pp. 115–44 in *Latin American Social Movements: Globalization, Democratization, and Transnational Networks*, edited by Hank Johnston and Paul Almeida. Lanham, MD: Rowman & Littlefield.

Boswell, Terry, and Christopher Chase-Dunn. 2000. *The Spiral of Capitalism and Socialism: Toward Global Democracy*. Boulder: Lynne Rienner.

Boxer, Marilyn J., and Jean H. Quataert. 1978. *Socialist Women: European Socialist Feminism in the Nineteenth and Early Twentieth Centuries*. New York: Elsevier.

Brim, Sand. 2003. "Report from Baghdad." *Off Our Backs* (March–April): 10–12.

Broad, Robin, ed. 2002. *Global Backlash: Citizen Initiatives for a Just World Economy*. Lanham, MD: Rowman & Littlefield.

Brown, Nathan, Amr Hamzawy, and Marina S. Ottaway. 2006. "Islamist Movements and the Democratic Process in the Arab World: Exploring Gray Zones." Washington, DC: Carnegie Endowment for International Peace, Paper No. 67 (March). http://www.carnegieendowment.org/files/cp_67_grayzones_final.pdf.

Bunch, Charlotte, and Roxanna Carillo. 1992. *Gender Violence: A Development and Human Rights Issue*. Dublin: Atlantic Press.

Cesari, Jocelyne. 2004. *When Islam and Democracy Meet: Muslims in Europe and in the United States*. New York: Palgrave Macmillan.

Chafetz, Janet S., and Gary Dworkin. 1986. *Female Revolt: Women's Movements in World and Historical Perspective*. Totowa, NJ: Rowman & Allanheld.

Chant, Sylvia. 1995. "Women's Roles in Recession and Economic Restructuring in Mexico and the Philippines." In *Poverty and Global Adjustment: The Urban Experience*, edited by Alan Gilbert. Oxford: Blackwell.

Chase-Dunn, Christopher. 1998. *Global Formation: Structures of the World Economy*. 2nd ed. Totowa, NJ: Rowman and Littlefield.

Chase-Dunn, Christopher, and Salvatore Babones, eds. 2006. *Global Social Change: Historical and Comparative Perspectives*. Baltimore: Johns Hopkins University Press.

Cherifati-Merabtine, Doria. 1995. "Algerian Women at a Crossroads: National Liberation, Islamization, and Women." Pp. 40–62 in *Gender and National Identity: Women and Politics in Muslim Societies*, edited by Valentine M. Moghadam. London: Zed Books

Chua, Amy. 2003. *World on Fire: How Exporting Free Market Democracy Breeds Ethnic Hatred and Global Instability*. New York: Doubleday.

Clark, Janine. 2004. *Islam, Charity and Activism: Middle-Class Networks and Social Welfare in Egypt, Jordan, and Yemen*. Bloomington: Indiana University Press.

Cohen, Robin, and Shirin M. Rai, eds. *Global Social Movements*. London: Athlone Press.

Connell, R. W. 1998. "Masculinities and Globalization." *Men and Masculinities* 1, no. 1: 1–20.

Cooley, John. 1999. *Unholy Wars: Afghanistan, America and International Terrorism*. London: Pluto Press.

Cox, Robert W. 1992. "Global Perestroika." Pp. 26–43 in *Socialist Register 1992*, edited by Ralph Miliband and Leo Panitch. London: Merlin Press.

Dahlerup, Drude, ed. 1987. *The New Women's Movement: Feminism and Political Power in Europe and the USA*. London: Sage.

della Porta, Donatella, ed. 2007. *The Global Justice Movement: Cross-National and Transnational Perspectives.* Boulder: Paradigm Publishers.

Dufour, Pascale, and Isabelle Giraud. 2007. "The Continuity of Transnational Solidarities in the World March of Women, 2000 and 2005: A Collective Identity-Building Approach." *Mobilization* 12, no. 3 (November): 307–22.

Dunaway, Wilma, ed. 2003a. *Emerging Issues in the Twenty-First Century World-System.* Vol. 1: *Crises and Resistance in the Twenty-First Century World-System.* Westport, CT: Praeger.

———, ed. 2003b. *Emerging Issues in the Twenty-First Century World-System.* Vol. 2: *New Theoretical Directions for the Twenty-First Century World-System.* Westport, CT: Praeger.

Eckstein, Susan E., and Timothy Wickham-Crowley. 2003. "Struggles for Social Rights in Latin America: Claims in the Arenas of Subsistence, Labor, Gender, and Ethnicity." Pp. 1–56 in *Struggles for Social Rights in Latin America*, edited by Susan E. Eckstein and Timothy Wickham-Crowley. London: Routledge.

Eisenstein, Zillah. 2004. *Against Empire: Feminisms, Racism, and the West.* London: Zed Books.

El-Ghobashy, Mona. 2005. "The Metamorphosis of the Egyptian Muslim Brothers." *International Journal of Middle East Studies* 37: 373–95.

Elson, Diane, and Ruth Pearson. 1981. "Nimble Fingers Make Cheap Workers: An Analysis of Women's Employment in Third World Export Manufacturing." *Feminist Review* (Spring): 87–107.

Enloe, Cynthia. 2007. *Globalization and Militarism: Feminists Make the Link.* Lanham, MD: Rowman & Littlefield.

———. 1990. *Bananas, Beaches and Bases: Making Feminist Sense of International Politics.* Berkeley: University of California Press.

Entelis, John. 2005. "Islamist Politics and the Democratic Imperative: Comparative Lessons from the Algerian Experience." In *Islam, Democracy and the State in Algeria: Lessons for the Western Mediterranean and Beyond*, edited by Michael D. Bonner, Megan Reif, and Mark Tessler. London: Routledge.

Esposito, John. 2002. *Unholy War: Terror in the Name of Islam.* Oxford: Oxford University Press.

———, ed. 1989. *The Iranian Revolution: Its Global Impact.* Gainesville: University Press of Florida.

Flam, Helena, and Debra King, eds. 2005. *Emotions and Social Movements.* New York: Routledge.

Flamhaft, Ziva. 2007. "Iron Breaks, Too: Israeli and Palestinian women talk about War, Bereaveament, and Peace." Pp. 311–26 in *From Patriarchy to Empowerment: Women's Participation, Movements, and Rights in the Middle East, North Africa, and South Asia*, edited by V. M. Moghadam. Syracuse, NY: Syracuse University Press.

Fourest, Caroline. 2004. *Frère Tariq: Discours, stratégie et méthode de Tariq Ramadan.* Paris: Grasset et Fasquelle.

Fraser, Arvonne. 1987. *The U.N. Decade for Women: Documents and Dialogue.* Boulder: Westview.

Frobel, Folker, Jurgen Jeinrichs, and Otto Kreye. 1980. *The New International Division of Labor.* Cambridge: Cambridge University Press.

Fukuyama, Francis. 1992. *The End of History and the Last Man.* New York: The Free Press.

Fuller, Graham. 2002. "The Future of Political Islam." *Foreign Affairs* (March/April): 48–60.

George, Susan. 2004. *Another World Is Possible If . . .* London: Verso.

Gerlach, Luther. 1999. "The Structure of Social Movements: Environmental Activism and Its Opponents." Pp. 85–98 in *Waves of Protest: Social Movements Since the Sixties*, edited by Jo Freeman and Victoria Johnson. Lanham, MD: Rowman & Littlefield.

Gerges, Fawaz. 2005. *The Far Enemy: Why Jihad Went Global.* Cambridge: Cambridge University Press.

Gills, Barry K., ed. 2000. *Globalization and the Politics of Resistance.* London: Macmillan.

Goodwin, Jeff. 2007. "Explaining Revolutionary Terrorism." Pp. 199–221 in *Revolution in the Making of the Modern World*, edited by John Foran, David Lane, and Andreja Zivkovic. London: Routledge.

———. 2001. *No Other Way Out: States and Revolutionary Movements, 1945–1991.* Cambridge: Cambridge University Press.

Goodwin, Jeff, James M. Jasper, and Francesca Polleta, eds. 2001. *Passionate Politics: Emotions and Social Movements.* Chicago: University of Chicago Press.

Guidry, John A., Michael D. Kennedy, and Mayer N. Zald, eds. 2000. *Globalizations and Social Movements: Culture, Power and the Transnational Public Sphere.* Ann Arbor: University of Michigan Press.

———. "Globalizations and Social Movements." Pp. 1–32 in *Globalizations and Social Movements: Culture, Power and the Transnational Public Sphere*, edited by John A. Guidry, Michael D. Kennedy, and Mayer N. Zald. Ann Arbor: University of Michigan Press.

Gulalp, Haldun. 2001. "Globalization and Political Islam: The Social Bases of Turkey's Welfare Party." *International Journal of Middle East Studies* 33: 433–48.

Hadden, Hennifer, and Sidney Tarrow. 2007. "The Global Justice Movement in the United States since Seattle." Pp. 210–31 in *The Global Justice Movement*, edited by Donatella della Porta.

Hafez, Mohammed. 2003. *Why Muslims Rebel: Repression and Resistance in the Islamic World.* Boulder: Lynne Rienner Publishers.

———. 2004. "From Marginalization to Massacres: A Political Process Explanation of GIA Violence in Algeria." Pp. 37–60 in *Islamic Activism: A Social Movement Theory Approach*, edited by Quintan Wictorowicz. Bloomington: Indiana University Press.

Hafez, Mohammed, and Quintan Wiktorowicz. 2004. "Violence as Contention in the Egyptian Islamic Movement." Pp. 61–88 in *Islamic Activism*, edited by Quintan Wictorowicz.

Halliday, Fred. 2005. *100 Myths About the Middle East*. London: Saqi.

Hamel, Pierre, Henri Lustiger-Thaler, Jan Nederveen Pieterse, and Sasha Roseneil, eds. 2001. *Globalization and Social Movements*. New York: Palgrave.

Hardt, Michael, and Antonio Negri. 2000. *Empire*. Cambridge, MA: Harvard University Press.

Harik, Judith. 2004. *Hezbollah: The Changing Face of Terrorism*. London: I.B. Taurus.

Harvey, David. 2004. "Neoliberalism and the Restoration of Class Power." *Via Portside* (August 6). http://www.portside.org.

———. 2003. *The New Imperialism*. Oxford: Oxford University Press.

Hawkesworth, Mary. 2006. *Globalization and Feminist Activism*. Lanham, MD: Rowman & Littlefield.

Heckscher, Zahara. 2002. "Long Before Seattle: Historical Resistance to Economic Globalization." Pp. 86–91 in *Global Backlash: Citizen Initiatives for a Just World Economy*, edited by Robin Broad. Lanham, MD: Rowman & Littlefield.

Held, David, ed. 2000. *A Globalizing World? Culture, Economics, Politics*. London: Routledge.

Hélie-Lucas, Marieme. 1993. "Women Living Under Muslim Laws." In *Ours by Right: Women's Rights as Human Rights*, edited by Joanna Kerr. London: Zed Books, in association with the North-South Institute.

Hirst, Paul, and Grahame Thompson. 1996. *Globalization in Question: The International Economy and the Possibilities of Governance*. Cambridge: Polity Press.

Hopkins, Terence K., and Immanuel Wallerstein. 1996. "The World System: Is There a Crisis?" Pp. 1–10 in *The Age of Transition: Trajectory of the World-System 1945–2025*, coordinated by Terence K. Hopkins et al. London: Zed.

Huntington, Samuel. 1996. *The Clash of Civilizations and the Remaking of World Order*. New York: Simon & Shuster.

Ibrahim, Saad Eddin. 1980. "Anatomy of Egypt's Militant Islamic Groups: Methodological Notes and Preliminary Findings." *International Journal of Middle East Studies* 12, no. 4 (December): 423–53.

International Gender and Trade Network. 2002. "With Women, Another World is Possible." IGTN statement, World Social Forum, Porto Alegre, Brazil (February). http://www.wide-network.org/index.jsp?id=198. (Last accessed January 16, 2008.)

Jayawardena, Kumari. 1986. *Feminism and Nationalism in the Third World*. London: Zed Books.

Johnson, Chalmers. 2001. "Blowback." *The Nation* (October 15). http://www.thenation.com/doc/20011015/johnson.

Johnston, Hank, and Paul Almeida, eds. 2006. *Latin American Social Movements*. Lanham, MD: Rowman & Littlefield.

Kaldor, Mary. 2003. *Global Civil Society: An Answer to War*. Cambridge: Polity Press.

Kandiyoti, Deniz, ed. 1991. *Women, Islam and the State*. London: Macmillan.

Kazi, Seema. 1997. "Muslim Laws and Women Living Under Muslim Laws." Pp. 141–146 in *Muslim Women and the Politics of Participation*, edited by Mahnaz Afkhami and Erika Friedl. Syracuse, NY: Syracuse University Press.

Keck, Margaret E., and Kathryn Sikkink. 2000. "Historical Precursors to Modern Transnational Social Movements and Networks." Pp. 35–53 in *Globalizations and Social Movements: Culture, Power and the Transnational Public Sphere*, edited by John A. Guidry, Michael D. Kennedy, and Mayer N. Zald. Ann Arbor: University of Michigan Press.

———. 1998. *Activists Beyond Borders: Advocacy Networks in International Politics*. Ithaca, NY: Cornell University Press.

Kepel, Gilles. 2002. *Jihad: The Trail of Political Islam*. Cambridge, MA: Harvard University Press.

Khosrokhavar, Farhad. 2005. *Suicide Bombers: Allah's New Martyrs*. Trans. David Macey. London: Pluto Press.

Klein, Naomi. 2007. *Shock Doctrine: The Rise of Disaster Capitalism*. New York: Henry Holt.

———. 2007b. "Latin America's Shock Resistance." *The Nation* (November 26). http://www.thenation.com/doc/20071126/klein.

Langman, Lauren. 2005. "From Virtual Public Spheres to Global Justice: A Critical Theory of Internetworked Social Movements." *Sociological Theory* 23, no. 1 (March): 42–74.

Langman, Lauren, and Douglas Morris. 2004. "Hegemony Lost: Understanding Contemporary Islam." In *Globalization, Hegemony and Power: Antisystemic Movements and the Global System*, edited by Thomas Reifer. Boulder: Paradigm.

Langman, Lauren, Douglas Morris, and Jackie Zalewski. 2002. "Globalization, Domination and Cyberactivism." In *The 21st Century World-System: Systemic Crises and Antisystemic Resistance*, edited by Wilma A. Dunaway. Westport, CT: Greenwood Press.

Langohr, Vickie. 2001. "Of Islamists and Ballot Boxes: Rethinking the Relationship between Islamisms and Electoral Politics." *International Journal of Middle East Studies* 33: 591–610.

Leatherman, Janie, and Julie A. Webber, eds. 2005. *Charting Transnational Democracy*. New York: Palgrave Macmillan.

Lizardo, Omar. 2006. "The Effect of Economic and Cultural Globalization on Anti-U.S. Transnational Terrorism 1971–2000." *Journal of World-Systems Research* 7, no. 1: 144–86.

Lycklama à Nijeholt, Geertje, Virginia Vargas, and Saskia Wieringa, eds. 1998. *Women's Movements and Public Policy in Europe, Latin America, and the Caribbean*. New York: Garland Publishing.

Marchand, Marianne, and Anne Sisson Runyan, eds. 2000. *Gender and Global Restructuring: Sightings, Sites and Resistances*. London: Routledge.

Marglin, Stephen, and Juliet Schor, eds. 1990. *The Golden Age of Capitalism*. Oxford: Clarendon Press.

Margolis, Diane. 1993. "Women's Movements Around the World: Cross-Cultural Comparisons." *Gender & Society* 7, no. 3 (September): 379–99.

Marty, Martin E., and R. Scott Appleby, eds. 1994. *The Fundamentalism Project*. Vol. 4: *Accounting for Fundamentalisms: The Dynamic Character of Movements*. Chicago: University of Chicago Press.

———. 1993. *The Fundamentalism Project*. Vol. 3: *Fundamentalisms and the State*. Chicago: University of Chicago Press.

———. 1992. *The Fundamentalism Project*. Vol. 2: *Fundamentalisms and Society*. Chicago: University of Chicago Press.

———. 1991. *The Fundamentalism Project*. Vol. 1: *Fundamentalisms Observed*. Chicago: University of Chicago Press.

Mathews, Jessica. 1997. "Power Shift." *Foreign Affairs* 76, no. 1 (January–February): 50–66.

McAdam, Doug, John McCarthy, and Meyer Zald, eds. 1996. *Comparative Perspectives on Social Movements: Political Opportunities, Mobilizing Structures, and Cultural Frames*. Cambridge: Cambridge University Press.

Melucci, Alberto. 1996. *Challenging Codes: Collective Action in the Information Age*. Cambridge: Cambridge University Press.

Mernissi, Fatima. 1987. *Beyond the Veil: Male-Female Dynamics in Modern Muslim Society*. Revised 2nd ed. Bloomington: Indiana University Press.

Mertes, Tom. 2004. "Grass-roots Globalism: Reply to Michael Hardt." Pp. 237–47 in *A Movement of Movements: Is Another World Really Possible?* edited by Tom Mertes. London: Verso.

Messaoudi, Khalida, and Elisabeth Schemla. 1995. *Unbowed: An Algerian Woman Confronts Islamic Fundamentalism*. Philadelphia: University of Pennsylvania Press.

Meyer, John, John Boli, George Thomas, Francisco Ramirez. 1997. "World Society and the Nation-State." *American Journal of Sociology* 103, no. 1:144–81.

Meyer, Mary K. 1999. "The Women's International League for Peace and Freedom: Organizing Women for Peace in the War System." Pp.107–21 in *Gender Politics in Global Governance*, edited by Mary K. Meyer and Elisabeth Prugl. Lanham, MD: Rowman & Littlefield.

Meyer, Mary K., and Elisabeth Prugl, eds. 1999. *Gender Politics in Global Governance*. Lanham, MD: Rowman & Littlefield.

Milanovic, Branko. 2005. *Worlds Apart: Measuring International and Global Inequality*. Princeton: Princeton University Press.

Milazzo, Linda. 2005. "Code Pink: The 21st Century Mothers of Invention." *Development* 48, no. 2: 100–104.

Mir-Hosseini, Ziba, and Richard Tapper. 2006. *Islam and Democracy in Iran: Eshkevari and the Quest for Reform*. London: I.B. Taurus.

Moaddel, Mansour. 2005. *Islamic Modernism, Nationalism, and Fundamentalism: Episode and Discourse*. Chicago: University of Chicago Press.

Moghadam, Valentine M. 2007. "Peace-building and Reconstruction with Women: Reflections on Afghanistan, Iraq, and Palestine." Pp. 327–51 in *From Patriarchy to Empowerment: Women's Participation, Movements, and Rights in the Middle East, North Africa, and South Asia*, edited by V. M. Moghadam. Syracuse, NY: Syracuse University Press.

———. 2005. *Globalizing Women: Gender, Globalization, and Transnational Feminist Networks*. Baltimore: Johns Hopkins University Press.

———. 2003. *Modernizing Women: Gender and Social Change in the Middle East*. 2nd ed. Boulder: Lynne Rienner.

———. 2001. "Organizing Women: The New Women's Movement in Algeria." *Cultural Dynamics* 13, number 2: 131–54.

———, ed. 1995. *Gender and National Identity: Women and Politics in Muslim Societies*. London: Zed Books.

———, ed. 1994. *Identity Politics and Women: Cultural Reassertions and Feminisms in International Perspective*. Boulder: Westview Press.

———, ed. 1993. *Democratic Reform and the Position of Women in Transitional Economies*. Oxford: Clarendon Press.

Munk, Ronaldo, ed. 2004. *Labour and Globalisation: Results and Prospects*. Liverpool University Press.

Munson, Henry, Jr. 1988. *Islam and Revolution in the Middle East*. New Haven: Yale University Press.

Naples, Nancy, and Manisha Desai, eds. 2002. *Women's Activism and Globalization*. London: Routledge.

Njehu, Njoki. 2004. "Cancel the Debt: Africa and the IMF." Pp. 94–110 in *A Movement of Movements: Is Another World Really Possible?* edited by Tom Mertes. London: Verso.

O'Brien, Robert, Anne Marie Goetz, Jan Aart Scholte, and Marc Williams. 2000. *Contesting Global Governance: Multilateral Economic Institutions and Global Social Movements*. Cambridge: Cambridge University Press.

Olesen, Thomas. 2007. "Contentious Cartoons: Elite and Media-Driven Mobilization." *Mobilization* 12, no. 1: 37–52.

Oxfam. 2002. *Rigged Rules and Double Standards: Trade, Globalization, and the Fight Against Poverty*. Oxford: Oxfam.

Pasha, Mustafa Kamal, and Ahmed I. Samatar. 1997. "The Resurgence of Islam." Pp. 187–201 in *Globalization: Critical Perspectives*, edited by James H. Mittelman. Boulder: Lynne Rienner Publishers.

Payer, Cheryl. 1975. *The Debt Trap: The International Monetary Fund and the Third World*. New York: Monthly Review Press.

Peterson, V. Spike. 2003. *A Critical Rewriting of Global Political Economy: Integrating Productive, Reproductive, and Virtual Economies*. New York: Routledge.

Pianta, Mario, and Raffaele Marchetti. 2007. "The Global Justice Movements: The Transnational Dimension." Pp. 29–51 in *The Global Justice Movement*, edited by Donatella della Porta.

Pieterse, Jan Nederveen. 2004. *Globalization or Empire?* London and New York: Routledge.

———. 1998. "Hybrid Modernities: Mélange Modernities in Asia." *Sociological Analysis* 1, no. 3: 75–86.

Pietila, Hilkka, and Jeanne Vickers. 1994. *Making Women Matter: The Role of the UN*. London: Zed.

Podobnik, Bruce. 2005. "Resistance to Globalization." Pp. 51–68 in *Transforming Globalization*. Edited by Bruce Podobnik and Thomas Reifer. Leiden, Netherlands: Brill Academic Publishers.

Podobnik, Bruce, and Thomas Ehrlich Reifer, eds. 2004. Special issue: *Global Social Movements Before and After 9-11. Journal of World Systems Research* 10, no. 1 (Winter). http://jwsr.ucr.edu/archive/vol10/number1.

Polanyi, Karl. 2001. *The Great Transformation: The Political and Economic Origins of Our Time*. Boston: Beacon Press.

Rahman, Fazlur. 1982. *Islam and Modernity: Transformation of an Intellectual Tradition*. Chicago: Publications of the Center for Middle Eastern Studies, University of Chicago.

Rashid, Ahmed. 2000. *Taliban: Militant Islam, Oil and Fundamentalism in Central Asia*. New Haven and London: Yale University Press.

Reardon, Betty. 1993. *Women and Peace: Feminist Visions of Global Security*. Albany: State University of New York Press.

Reese, Ellen, Erika Gutierrez, and Christopher Chase-Dunn. 2007. "Labor and Other Anti-systemic Movements in the World Social Forum Process." IROWS Working Paper #17. http://irows.ucr.edu.

Reid, Edna, and Hsinchen Chen. 2007. "Internet-Savvy U.S. and Middle Eastern Extremist Groups." *Mobilization* 12, no. 2 (June): 177–92.

Roberts, J. Timmons, and Amy Bellone Hite, eds. 2007. *The Globalization and Development Reader*. London: Blackwell Publishers

Robinson, William I. 2004. *A Theory of Global Capitalism*. Baltimore: Johns Hopkins University Press.

Robinson, William I., and Jerry Harris. 2000. "Towards a Global Class? Globalization and the Transnational Capitalist Class." *Science & Society* 64, no. 1 (Spring): 11–54.

Round, Robin. 2004. "Controlling Casino Capitalism." Pp. 282–86 in *Global Backlash: Citizen Initiatives for a Just World Economy*, edited by Robin Broad. Lanham, MD: Rowman & Littlefield.

Roy, Olivier. 2004. *Globalized Islam: The Search for a New Ummah*. New York: Columbia University Press.

Rubin, Barnett. 1997. "Arab Islamists in Afghanistan." Pp. 179–206 in *Political Islam: Revolution, Radicalism, or Reform?* edited by John Esposito. Boulder: Lynne Rienner Publishers.

Rueschemeyer, Marilyn, ed. 1998. *Women in the Politics of Postcommunist Eastern Europe*. Armonk, New York: M.E. Sharpe.

Rupert, Mark, and M. Scott Solomon. 2006. *Globalization and International Political Economy*. Lanham, MD: Rowman & Littlefield.

Rupp, Leila. 1998. *Worlds of Women: The Making of an International Women's Movement*. Princeton: Princeton University Press.

Salamé, Ghassan, ed. 1994. *Democracy without Democrats: The Renewal of Politics in the Muslim World*. London: I.B. Taurus.

Santos, Boaventura de Sousa. 2006. *The Rise of the Global Left: The World Social Forum and Beyond*. London: Zed Books.

Scholte, Jan Aart. 2000. *Globalization: A Critical Introduction*. London: Palgrave.

Schwedler, Jillian. 2006. *Faith in Moderation: Islamist Parties in Jordan and Yemen*. New York: Cambridge University Press.

Shaheed, Farida. 1994. "Controlled or Autonomous: Identity and the Experience of the Network Women Living Under Muslim Laws." WLUML Occasional Paper No. 5 (July).

Shiva, Vandana. 2000. "War against Nature and the People of the South." Pp. 91–124 in *Views from the South: The Effects of Globalization and the WTO on Third World Countries*, edited by Sarah Anderson. Chicago: Food First and the International Forum on Globalization.

Sidahmed, A. Salam, and Anoushirvan Ehteshami, eds. 1996. *Islamic Fundamentalism*. Boulder: Westview.

Sklair, Leslie. 2002. *Globalization: Capitalism and Its Alternatives*. 3rd ed. Oxford: Oxford University Press.

———. 2001. *The Transnational Capitalist Class*. Oxford: Blackwell Publishers

———. 1991. *A Sociology of the Global System*. Baltimore: Johns Hopkins University Press.

Smith, Jackie, Charles Chatfield, and Ron Pagnucco, eds. 1997. *Transnational Social Movements and Global Politics*. Syracuse, NY: Syracuse University Press.

Smith, Jackie, and Hank Johnston, eds. 2002. *Globalization and Resistance: Transnational Dimensions of Social Movements*. Lanham, MD: Rowman & Littlefield.

Smith, Jackie, Marina Karides, Marc Becker, Dorval Brunelle, Christopher Chase-Dunn, Rosalba Icaza, Jeffrey Juris, Lorenzo Mosca, Donatella della Porta, Ellen Reese, Peter Jay Smith, and Rolando Vásquez. 2008. *The World Social Forums and the Challenge of Global Democracy*. Boulder: Paradigm Publishers.

Smith, Jackie, and Dawn Wiest. 2005. "The Uneven Geography of Global Civil Society: National and Global Influences on Transnational Association." *Social Forces* 84: 621–51.

Snow, David A. 2004. "Framing Processes, Ideology, and Discursive Fields." Pp. 380–412 in *The Blackwell Companion to Social Movements*, edited by David A. Snow, Sarah Soule, and Hanspieter Kriesi. Malden, MA: Blackwell.

Sperling, Valerie, Myra Marx Ferree, and Barbara Risman. 2001. "Constructing Global Feminism: Transnational Advocacy Networks and Russian Women's Activism." *Signs* 26, no. 4: 1155–86.

Standing, Guy. 1999. "Global Feminization Through Flexible Labor: A Theme Revisited." *World Development* 27, no. 3: 583–602.

———. 1989. "Global Feminization through Flexible Labor." *World Development* 17, no. 7): 1077–95.

Starhawk. 2003. "Why We Need Women's Actions and Feminist Voices for Peace." *Off Our Backs* (March–April): 16–17.

Steger, Manfred. 2003. *Globalization: A Very Short Introduction.* Oxford: Oxford University Press.

———. 2002. *Globalism.* Lanham, MD: Rowman & Littlefield.

Stienstra, Deborah. 2000. "Dancing Resistance from Rio to Beijing: Transnational Women's Organizing and United Nations Conferences, 1992–1996." Pp. 209–224 in *Gender and Global Restructuring: Sightings, Sites and Resistances,* edited by Anne Sisson Runyan and Marianne Marchand. London: Routledge.

———. 1994. *Women's Movements and International Organizations.* New York: St. Martin's Press.

Strange, Susan. 1996. *The Retreat of the State: The Diffusion of Power in the World Economy.* Cambridge: Cambridge University Press.

Subcomandante Marcos. 2004. "The Hourglass of the Zapatistas." Interview with Gabriel García Márquez and Roberto Pombo. Pp. 3–15 in *A Movement of Movements: Is Another World Really Possible?* edited by Tom Mertes. London: Verso.

Tarrow, Sidney. 2005. *The New Transnational Activism.* Cambridge: Cambridge University Press.

———. 2001. "Transnational Politics: Contention and Institutions in International Politics." *Annual Review of Political Science* 4: 1–20.

Taylor, Lance. 2000. "External Liberalization, Economic Performance, and Distribution in Latin America and Elsewhere." Helsinki: WIDER Working Papers No. 215 (December).

———. 1993. *The Rocky Road to Reform: Adjustment, Income Distribution and Growth in the Developing World.* Cambridge, MA: MIT Press.

Taylor, Rupert. 2004. "Interpreting Global Civil Society." Pp. 2–10 in *Creating a Better World: Interpreting Global Civil Society,* edited by Rupert Taylor. Bloomfield, CT: Kumarian Press.

Tickner, Ann. 1992. *Gender in International Relations: Feminist Perspectives on Achieving Global Security.* New York: Columbia University Press.

UNDP. 1999. *Human Development Report 1999* [on globalization]. New York: Oxford University Press.

Vargas, Virginia. 2005. "Feminisms and the World Social Forum: Space for Dialogue and Confrontation." *Development* 48, no. 2: 107–10.

Waddington, David, and Mike King. 2007. "The Impact of the Local: Police Public-Order Strategies during the G8 Justice and Home Affairs Ministerial Meetings." *Mobilization* 12, no. 4 (December): 417–30.

Wallerstein, Immanuel. 2003. *The Decline of American Power: The U.S. in a Chaotic World.* New York: New Press.

———. 2000. "Globalization or the Age of Transition? A Long-Term View of the Trajectory of the World-System." *International Sociology* 15, no. 2: 249–65.

———. 1991.*Geopolitics and Geoculture: Essays on the Changing World-system.* Cambridge: Cambridge University Press.

Walton, John, and David Seddon. 1994. *Free Markets and Food Riots: The Politics of Global Adjustment.* Oxford: Blackwell.

Waterman, Peter. 1998. *Globalization, Social Movements and the New Internationalisms.* London: Marshall.

West, Guida, and Rhoda Blumberg, eds. 1990. *Women and Social Protest.* New York: Oxford University Press.

Wichterich, Christa. 1999. *The Globalized Woman: Notes from a Future of Inequality.* London: Zed Books.

WIDE. 1998. *Trade Traps and Gender Gaps: Women Unveiling the Market.* Report on WIDE's Annual Conference held at Jarvenpaa, Finland, May 16–18, 1997. Brussels: Women in Development Europe.

Wiest, Dawn. 2007. "A Story of Two Transnationalisms: Global Salafi Jihad and Transnational Human Rights Mobilization in the Middle East and North Africa." *Mobilization* 12, no. 2 (June): 137–60.

Wiktorowicz, Quintan. 2005. *Radical Islam Rising: Muslim Extremism in the West.* Lanham, MD: Rowman & Littlefield.

———. 2004. "Introduction: Islamic Activism and Social Movement Theory." Pp. 1–36 in *Islamic Activism*, edited by Quintan Wiktorowicz.

———, ed. 2004. *Islamic Activism: A Social Movement Theory Approach.* Bloomington: Indiana University Press.

WLUML. 2005. "WLUML Appeal Against Fundamentalisms: There Is No Such Thing As the 'Clash of Civilizations': The Clash in the World Today Is Between Fascists and Antifascists." http://www.wluml.org/english/newsfulltxt.shtml ?cmd%5B157%5D=x-157-103376. (Last accessed January 16, 2008.)

Yaghmaian, Behzad. 2001. "The Political Economy of Global Accumulation and Its Emerging Mode of Regulation." In *Labor and Capital in the Age of Globalization: The Labor Process and the Changing Nature of Work in the Global Economy*, edited by Berch Berberoglu. Lanham, MD: Rowman & Littlefield.

Young, Kate, ed. 1992. *Gender and Development Reader.* Ottawa: Canadian Council for International Cooperation.

Zivkovic, Andrea, and John Hogan. 2007. "Virtual Revolution? ICTs and Networks." Pp. 182–98 in *Revolution in the Making of the Modern World*, edited by John Foran, David Lane, and Andreja Zivkovic. London: Routledge.

Zubaida, Sami. 1993. *Islam, the People and the State: Political Ideas and Movements in the Middle East.* London: I.B. Taurus.

INDEX

Page references in *italics* indicate a figure or table.

ABOUT THE AUTHOR

Valentine M. Moghadam joined Purdue University in January 2007 as professor of sociology and women's studies and director of the Women's Studies Program. From May 2004 to December 2006 she was chief of the Section for Gender Equality and Development, Social and Human Sciences Sector of UNESCO, in Paris, France. Her work at UNESCO involved networking with and capacity building of women's organizations, as well as policy-oriented research on globalization and women's human rights, cultures and gender equality, and the gender dynamics of conflict, peace, and reconstruction. She helped establish the Palestinian Women's Research and Documentation Center in Ramallah, Palestinian Authority. Prior to that, she was director of women's studies and professor of sociology at Illinois State University.

Born in Tehran, Iran, Dr. Moghadam received her higher education in Canada and the United States. After obtaining her Ph.D. in sociology from the American University in Washington, D.C., in 1986, she taught the sociology of development and women in development at New York University. From 1990 through 1995 she was senior researcher and coordinator of the Research Program on Women and Development at the WIDER Institute of the United Nations University (UNU/WIDER) and was based in Helsinki, Finland. She was a member of the UNU delegation to the World Summit on Social Development (Copenhagen, March 1995) and the Fourth World Conference on Women (Beijing, September 1995).

Dr. Moghadam is author of *Modernizing Women: Gender and Social Change in the Middle East* (1993; second edition 2003) and *Women, Work and Economic Reform in the Middle East and North Africa* (1998). Her third book, *Globalizing Women: Transnational Feminist Networks*, won the APSA's 2005 Victoria Schuck Award for best book on women and politics. Her edited volumes include *From Patriarchy to Empowerment: Participation, Rights, and Women's Movements in the Middle East, North Africa and South Asia* (2007) and (with Massoud Karshenas) *Social Policy in the Middle East: Economic, Political, and Gender Dynamics* (2006).

Dr. Moghadam's areas of research are globalization, transnational feminist networks, civil society and citizenship, and women's employment in the Middle East. She has lectured and published widely and served as a consultant for many international organizations. She is a contributor to a 2001 report, coordinated by CAWTAR and the UNDP, on the impact of globalization on women's economic conditions in the Arab world. She also prepared a background paper on Islam, culture, and women's rights in the Middle East for the UNDP's *Human Development Report 2004*.